MATH PRACTICE WORKBOOK

GRADES 4-5

P9-AQD-149

BRAIN HUNTER

1000+ QUESTIONS YOU NEED TO KILL IN ⟹ **ELEMENTARY SCHOOL**

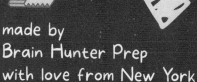

made by
Brain Hunter Prep
with love from New York

Books made by Brain Hunter Prep
with love from New York

GRADE 1-3

GRADE 4-5
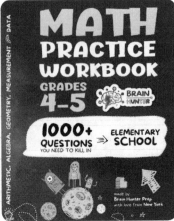

GRADE 6-8

We take great pride in providing our students, parents, and educators with the best educational products and customer service. We kindly ask for one minute of your time to leave us an honest review on Amazon for this workbook.

Reviews help us grow our brand, improve our products, and allow customers to learn more about our workbooks. Thanks for letting us be a part of your child's educational journey.

ALL RIGHTS RESERVED
Copyright © 2022 by Brain Hunter Prep Inc.

ISBN-13: 9781951048235
Published by Brain Hunter Prep Inc.

All rights reserved, no part of this book may be reproduced or distributed in any form or by any means without the written permi..... in ......er Prep Inc.
All the materials within are the exclusive property of Brain Hunter Prep Inc.

TABLE OF CONTENTS

OTHER BOOKS BY ARGOPREP

Here are some other test prep workbooks by ArgoPrep you may be interested in. All of our workbooks come equipped with detailed video explanations to make your learning experience a breeze! Visit us at **www.argoprep.com**

COMMON CORE MATH SERIES

COMMON CORE ELA SERIES

INTRODUCING MATH!

Introducing Math! by ArgoPrep is an award-winning series created by certified teachers to provide students with high-quality practice problems. Our workbooks include topic overviews with instruction, practice questions, answer explanations along with digital access to video explanations. Practice in confidence - with ArgoPrep!

   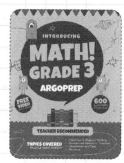 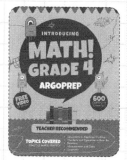

   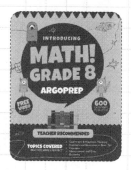 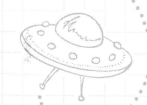

SCIENCE SERIES

Science Daily Practice Workbook by ArgoPrep is an award-winning series created by certified science teachers to help build mastery of foundational science skills. Our workbooks explore science topics in depth with ArgoPrep's 5 E's to build science mastery.

KIDS SUMMER ACADEMY SERIES

ArgoPrep's **Kids Summer Academy** series helps prevent summer learning loss and gets students ready for their new school year by reinforcing core foundations in math, english and science. Our workbooks also introduce new concepts so students can get a head start and be on top of their game for the new school year!

Want much more free worksheets?

Visit us at argoprep.com/worksheets

Arithmetic

1. The junior class is raising money for the prom. They will sell Candy Grams and need to put a chocolate on 1200 valentines. The class has already placed the chocolates on 766 valentines. How many more chocolates do they need to place on the valentines?

   A. 1966
   B. 443
   C. 434
   D. 344

   Difficulty: Easy

2. Elise and Sarah are designing a necklace and need 86 beads. They have 22 red beads, 25 blue beads, and 35 white beads. How many more beads do the girls need to finish the necklace?

   E. 4
   F. 2
   G. 5
   H. 3

   Difficulty: Hard

3. Franz grew 31 cucumbers, Jose grew 26 cucumbers, and Antonio grew 29 cucumbers. How many cucumbers did they grow in total?

   A. 68
   B. 85
   C. 88
   D. 86

   Difficulty: Moderate

4. Rene had 15 baseball cards. Reynaldo gave him 11 new baseball cards. Julian bought 18 baseball cards. How many baseball cards does Rene have now ?

   E. 44
   F. 26
   G. 33
   H. 29

   Difficulty: Hard

5. Trent had 20 nickels and 40 quarters in his bank. His dad gave him 20 quarters and his mother gave him 45 nickels. How many nickels does Trent have now?

   A. 125
   B. 60
   C. 105
   D. 65

   Difficulty: Hard

6. Madeline went to 12 football games this year, but missed 4. She went to 13 games last year and plans to go to 16 games next year. How many total football games will Madeline go to?

   E. 41
   F. 45
   G. 25
   H. 37

   Difficult: Moderate

7. Gabriel had **35** marbles in his collection. His dad gave him **12** more but he lost **2** of them. How many marbles does Gabriel have now?

A.) 49   C. 37

B. 14   D. 45

$$\begin{array}{r} 35 \\ +12 \\ \hline 47 \\ +2 \\ \hline 49 \end{array}$$

Difficulty: Hard

8. Lindsay found **14** shark's teeth while her sister, Kristen, found **19**, and her brother, Scott, found **17** on the beach. How many shark's teeth did they find together?

E. 33   G.) 50

F. 31   H. 36

$$\begin{array}{r} 19 \\ +17 \\ \hline 36 \\ +14 \\ \hline 50 \end{array}$$

Difficulty: Moderate

9. James and Mark have picked **98** apples and **67** pears. They drop the barrel of apples and **17** are lost. How many apples and pears did James and Mark finally have?

A. 165   C.) 148

B. 115   D. 146

$$\begin{array}{r} 98 \\ +67 \\ \hline 165 \\ -17 \\ \hline 148 \end{array}$$

Difficulty: Hard

10. Last year, Anders checked out **37** books from his local library. Raul checked out **25**. Jackson lost **2** of the **29** he had checked out. How many books did the three boys check out in total?

E.) 93   G. 95

F. 91   H. 89

$$\begin{array}{r} 64 \\ +29 \\ \hline 93 \end{array}$$

$$\begin{array}{r} 37 \\ +25 \\ \hline 62 \\ +2 \\ \hline 64 \end{array}$$

Difficulty: Hard

11. What number has **2** hundreds, **7** tens, and **6** ones?

A. 267   C. 672

B. 726   D.) 276

Difficulty: Easy

12. What number is equal to **800 + 60 + 4**?

E. 648   G. 468

F.) 864   H. 846

Difficulty: Easy

13. How many hundreds are in the number **948**?

A.) 9   C. 2

B. 8   D. 4

Difficulty: Easy

1. Darcy has thirty-seven green balloons, Lauryn has fifteen green balloons, and Meagan has thirty-eight green balloons. The balloons cost twenty-seven dollars. How many green balloons do they have in all?

E. 52

G. 90

F. 80

H. 63

37
+15
152
+38
90

Difficulty: Hard

2. What place value is 2 in the number 218,379?

A. thousands
B. hundreds
C. ten thousands
D. hundred thousands

Difficulty: Easy

3. What is the value of 0 in the number, 584,098?

E. 100

G. 0

F. 10

H. 1

Difficulty: Easy

4. Use place values to solve:
1,200 ÷ 30 = ____

A. 4

C. 400

B. 40

D. 4000

Difficulty: Moderate

5. Use place value to solve:
20 × 70 = ____

E. 14

G. 1,400

F. 140

H. 14,000

Difficulty: Moderate

6. In the number, 379,292, the 9 in the thousands place is _____ the value of the 9 in the tens place.

A. 1 x

C. 100 x

B. 10 x

D. 1000 x

Difficulty: Hard

7. In the number, 4,118, the 1 in the tens place is _____ the value of the 1 in the hundreds place.

E. 100

G. 1

F. 10

H. $\frac{1}{10}$

Difficulty: Hard

8. Use place value to solve:
90 × 60 = ____

A. 540

C. 54

B. 5,400

D. 54,000

Difficulty: Moderate

9. Use place value to solve:
2,700 ÷ 90 = ____.

E. 30   G. 300

F. 3   H. 10

Difficulty: Moderate

10. Which is the place value of the **3** in the number 9,365,412?

A. thousands
B. tens
C. hundred thousands
D. ones

Difficulty: Moderate

11. Which of the following is the correct order of the missing numbers in nine thousand twenty seven?

____ thousands + ____ hundreds + ____ tens + ____ ones

E. 9,127   G. 90,027

F. 927   H. 9,027

Difficulty: Moderate

12. Which of the following is the correct order of the missing numbers in sixty thousand four?

____ ten thousands + ____ thousands + ____ hundreds + ____ tens + ____ ones

A. 60,004   C. 604

B. 64,000   D. 60,400

Difficulty: Hard

13. Since she was hired, a chef has served **521** adults and **705** children. What is the total number of guests served?

E. 184   G. 126

F. 1,026   H. 1,226

Difficulty: Easy

14. Susan planted **25** tulips, **30** day lilies, and **15** irises. How many flowers did Susan plant in all?

A. 70   C. 66

B. 59   D. 56

Difficulty: Hard

1. What is the place value of the underlined number in 8̲90,146?

   E. thousands
   F. hundreds
   G. hundred thousands
   H. ten thousands

   Difficulty: Moderate

2. Which is the place value of the 3 in the number 23,674?

   A. hundreds
   B. thousands
   C. ten thousands
   D. tens

   Difficulty: Moderate

3. Using the numbers: 3 , 0 , 8. What is the smallest number you can create?

   E. 0   G. 30
   F. 083   H. 038

   Difficulty: Hard

4. Using the numbers: 5 , 1 , 8. What number can you make that is smaller than 185?

   A. 18   C. 15
   B. 185   D. 158

   Difficulty: Hard

5. What is the value of the 6 in the number 89,264,815?

   E. millions
   F. hundred thousands
   G. ten thousands
   H. thousands

   Difficulty: Moderate

6. Which choice has a 3 with the value of 30,000 or 3 ten thousands?

   A. 56,639   C. 35,165
   B. 94,953   D. 278,973

   Difficulty: Moderate

7. Which choice has a 6 with the value of 60 or 6 tens?

   E. 169   G. 456
   F. 684   H. 603

   Difficulty: Moderate

8. What is the value of the 9 in the number 8,591,503?

   A. hundred thousands
   B. ten thousands
   C. thousands
   D. hundreds

   Difficulty: Moderate

9. Pedro goes to the fruit stand and buys strawberries, bananas, and peaches. The fruit will last Pedro for 7 days. He buys 11 strawberries, 4 bananas, and 12 peaches. How many pieces of fruit does Pedro buy in all?

E. 20   G. 26

F. 27   H. 22

Difficulty: Hard

10. Caroline drove 18 kilometers from her house to Spartanburg. Spartanburg is 6 kilometers north of Easley. From Spartanburg, Caroline drove 11 kilometers to Greenville. Then she drove 12 kilometers from Greenville to Simpsonville. How far did Caroline drive in all, from her house to Simpsonville?

A. 30   C. 35

B. 42   D. 41

Difficulty: Hard

11. In 216.9658, in which place is the 9?

E. tenths
F. tens
G. thousandths
H. hundreds

Difficulty: Hard

12. In the number, 863,083.249, what place is the 4 in?

A. tenths
B. ones
C. hundredths
D. thousandths

Difficulty: Hard

13. What number has 8 hundreds, 0 tens, and 2 ones?

E. 208   G. 820

F. 802   H. 82

Difficulty: Easy

14. What number is equal to 600 + 20 + 9?

A. 620   C. 926

B. 692   D. 629

Difficulty: Easy

15. Anna read 21 pages of her novel on Monday, 19 on Tuesday, and 17 on Thursday. She went for a walk on Wednesday and Friday. How many pages did Anna read?

E. 57   G. 56

F. 55   H. 54

Difficulty: Hard

1. What digit is in the millions place in the number 4,821,753?

   A. 5   C. 1
   B. 4   D. 2

   Difficulty: Moderate

2. What digit is in the hundred thousands place in the number 2,948,675?

   E. 2   G. 8
   F. 6   H. 9

   Difficulty: Moderate

3. 216,367.52 The 2 in the hundred thousands place is _____ the value of the 2 in the hundredths place.

   A. 1,000,000 ×
   B. 100,000 ×
   C. 10,000,000 ×
   D. $\frac{1}{10,000,000}$ ×

   Difficulty: Hard

4. 3,364,761.3 The 6 in the tens place is _____ the value of the 6 in the ten thousands place.

   E. $\frac{1}{1000}$ G. 1,000 ×

   F. $\frac{1}{10,000}$ H. 100 ×

   Difficulty: Hard

5. 1,800 ÷ 90 = ____

   A. 2   C. 200
   B. 20   D. 90

   Difficulty: Moderate

6. Liam bought **2** movies to watch on Tuesday during his break. Then he bought **2** boxes of popcorn, **2** bottles of pop, and **2** boxes of candy. Thursday he decided to buy **2** more movies and then again on Saturday, he bought **3** more movies. How many movies did Liam buy in total during his break?

E. 4   G. 6

F. 7   H. 13

Difficulty: Hard

7. The science club was selling raffle tickets as a fund raiser for the science department. Angie sold **22** tickets and Pam sold 19. John lost 4 of his but sold a total of 11. How many raffle tickets were sold in all?

A. 60   C. 41

B. 52   D. 59

Difficulty: Hard

8. Which of the following is the correct order of the missing numbers in sixty thousand fifty six?

____ ten thousands + ____ thousands + ____ hundreds + ____ tens + ____ ones

E. 60,056   G. 60,560

F. 6,056   H. 60,650

Difficulty: Moderate

1. Which of the following is the standard form of the number, forty-two thousand, three hundred forty-eight?

A. 4,348   **C.** 24,348

B. 42,438   **D.** 42,348

Difficulty: Easy

2. Which of the following is the standard form of the number, seven thousand, two hundred forty?

E. 70, 240   **G.** 724

F. 7,240   **H.** 700,240

Difficulty: Easy

3. Which of the following is the written form of the number, 20,080?

A. twenty thousand eighty
B. twenty thousand eight hundred
C. twenty thousand eight
D. two thousand eight

Difficulty: Easy

4. Which of the following is the written form of the number, 246,742?

E. two hundred forty-seven thousand, six hundred forty-two
F. two hundred forty-six thousand, seven hundred forty
G. two hundred forty thousand, seven hundred forty-two
H. two hundred forty-six thousand, seven hundred forty-two

Difficulty: Easy

5. Which of the following is the standard form of the number, eight hundred twenty-seven thousand, three hundred ninety-one?

A. 927,381   **C.** 827,391

B. 927,391   **D.** 827,381

Difficulty: Easy

6. Which of the following is the standard form of the number, seven hundred eighty-four thousand twenty?

E. 784,020   **G.** 784,200

F. 786,020   **H.** 784,002

Difficulty: Easy

7. Which of the following is the correct expanded form of the number, three thousand, three hundred seventy-two?

A. $3000 + 300 + 70 + 2$
B. $3000 + 300 + 2$
C. $3000 + 300 + 70$
D. $3000 + 200 + 70 + 3$

Difficulty: Moderate

8. What is the word form of $7000 + 30 + 1$?

E. seven thousand one hundred thirty-one
F. seven thousand thirty-one
G. seven hundred thirty-one
H. seven thousand three hundred one

Difficulty: Moderate

9. What is the standard form of $200,000 + 200$?

A. 220,000
B. 202,000
C. 200,200
D. 200,020

Difficulty: Hard

10. What is the standard form of three thousand thirty-one?

E. 30,031
F. 301
G. 31
H. 3,031

Difficulty: Hard

11. What is the standard form of one hundred seventy-seven thousand, five hundred sixty-three?

A. 17,563
B. 170,563
C. 177,563
D. 177,365

Difficulty: Hard

12. Which of the following is the expanded form of the number, 40,870?

A. $40,000 + 800 + 70$
B. $40,000 + 80 + 7$
C. $4,000 + 800 + 70$
D. $4,000 + 80 + 8$

Difficulty: Hard

13. Which of the following is the expanded form of the number, 30,970?

E. $3,000 + 900 + 7$
F. $30,000 + 900 + 70$
G. $3,000 + 900 + 70$
H. $30,000 + 90 + 7$

Difficulty: Hard

1. Which of the following is the expanded form of the number, 983,546,917?

   A. 900,000,000 + 80,000,000 + 3,000,000 + 500,000 + 40,000 + 6,000 + 900 + 10 + 7

   B. 900,000,000 + 80,000,000 + 3,000,000 + 50,000 + 4,000 + 6,000 + 900 + 10 + 7

   C. 900,000,000 + 8,000,000 + 3,000,000 + 500,000 + 40,000 + 6,000 + 900 + 10 + 7

   D. 90,000,000 + 8,000,000 + 3,000,000 + 500,000 + 40,000 + 6,000 + 900 + 10 + 7

   Difficulty: Hard

2. What is the expanded form of the number, 6,142,917?

   E. 6,000,000 + 100,000 + 40,000 + 200 + 900 + 10 + 7

   F. 6,000,000 + 100,000 + 4,000 + 2,000 + 900 + 10 + 7

   G. 6,000,000 + 100,000 + 40,000 + 2,000 + 900 + 10 + 7

   H. 6,000,000 + 10,000 + 40,000 + 2,000 + 900 + 10 + 7

   Difficulty: Hard

3. What is the standard form of 9 ten thousands + 9 thousands + 1 hundred + 4 tens + 7 ones?

   A. 990,147   C. 9,147

   B. 99,147   D. 947

   Difficulty: Moderate

4. What is the standard form of 6 hundred thousands + 7 ten thousands + 4 thousands + 2 hundreds + 3 tens + 1 one?

   E. 674,031   G. 604,231

   F. 674,231   H. 674,200

   Difficulty: Hard

5. Which of the following is the expanded form of the number, 805,942,730,314?

A. 8 hundred billions + 5 billions + 9 ten millions + 4 millions + 2 millions + 7 hundred thousands + 3 ten thousands + 3 hundreds + 1 ten + 4 ones

B. 8 hundred billions + 5 billions + 9 hundred millions + 4 ten millions + 2 millions + 7 hundred thousands + 3 ten thousands + 3 hundreds + 1 ten + 4 ones

C. 8 hundred billions + 5 billions + 9 hundred millions + 4 ten millions + 2 millions + 7 hundred thousands + 3 thousands + 3 hundreds + 4 ones

D. 8 hundred billions + 5 billions + 9 hundred millions + 4 millions + 2 millions + 7 hundreds + 3 ten thousands + 3 hundreds + 1 ten + 4 ones

Difficulty: Hard

6. What is the expanded form of the number, 53,089,260?

E. 5 ten millions + 3 millions + 8 ten thousands + 9 thousands + 2 hundreds + 6 tens

F. 5 ten millions + 3 millions + 9 thousands + 2 hundreds + 6 tens

G. 5 ten millions + 3 millions + 8 ten thousands + 9 thousands + 6 tens

H. 5 ten millions + 3 millions + 8 ten thousands + 9 thousands + 2 hundreds

Difficulty: Hard

7. What is the standard form of the number, 600,000 + 50,000 + 4,000 + 500 + 80 + 6?

A. 654,586,000
B. 6,586
C. 654,586
D. 6,540,586

Difficulty: Hard

1. Which of the following is the correct expanded form of 7,871,640?

   E. 7,000,000 + 800,000 + 70,000+ 1,000 + 600+ 40+ 2

   F. 7,000,000 + 800,000 + 70,000+ 1,000 + 600+ 40

   G. 7,000,000 + 800,000 + 70,000+ 1,000 + 600+ 0

   H. 7,000,000 + 800,000 + 70,000 + 600+ 40+ 0

   Difficulty: Hard

2. Which of the following is the correct standard form of the number, 10,000 + 6,000 + 800 + 10 + 7?

   A. 16,817   C. 16,017

   B. 1,817   D. 1,687

   Difficulty: Moderate

3. Which of the following is the correct expanded form of the number, 6,457,326?

   E. (6 x 1,000,000) + (4 x 100,000) + (5 x 10,000) + (7 x 1,000) + (3 x 100) + (2 x 10) + (6 x 1)

   F. (6 x 1,000,000) + (4 x 100,000) + (5 x 10,000) + (7 x 1,000) + (3 x 100) + (6 x 1)

   G. (6 x 1,000,000) + (4 x 100,000) + (5 x 10,000) + (3 x 100) + (2 x 10) + (6 x 1)

   H. (6 x 1,000,000) + (4 x 100,000) + (7 x 1,000) + (3 x 100) + (3 x 10) + (6 x 1)

   Difficulty: Hard

4. Which of the following is the correct standard number for forty-five thousand thirty?

   A. 4,530   C. 45,030

   B. 4,503   D. 45,330

   Difficulty: Moderate

5. Which of the following is the correct standard number for nine thousand, five hundred twenty?

   E. 9,052   G. 9,522

   F. 952   H. 9,520

   Difficulty: Moderate

6. Which of the following is the word form of the number, 902,140?

   A. nine hundred two thousand, one hundred four

   B. nine hundred two thousand, one hundred forty

   C. nine hundred two thousand, four hundred forty

   D. nine hundred thousand, one hundred forty

   Difficulty: Hard

7. Which of the following is the word form of the number, 2,431?

   E. two thousand, four hundred thirty

   F. two thousand, three hundred forty-one

   G. two thousand, four hundred thirty-one

   H. four thousand, two hundred thirty-one

   Difficulty: Moderate

8. Which of the following is the expanded form of the number, 6,790,520?

   A. $(6 \times 1{,}000{,}000) + (7 \times 100{,}000) + (0 \times 1{,}000) + (5 \times 100) + (2 \times 10) + (0 \times 1)$

   B. $(6 \times 1{,}000{,}000) + (7 \times 100{,}000) + (9 \times 10{,}000) + (0 \times 1{,}000) + (5 \times 100) + (2 \times 10) + (0 \times 1)$

   C. $(6 \times 1{,}000{,}000) + (7 \times 100{,}000) + (9 \times 10{,}000) + (0 \times 1{,}000) + (2 \times 10) + (0 \times 1)$

   D. $(6 \times 1{,}000{,}000) + (7 \times 1{,}000{,}000) + (9 \times 10{,}000) + (5 \times 100) + (2 \times 10)$

   Difficulty: Hard

9. The correct word form of the number, 121,835 is _____.

   E. one hundred twenty-one thousand, eight thirty-five

   F. one hundred twenty-one, eight hundred thirty-five

   G. one hundred twenty-one, eight hundred thirty-five thousand

   H. one hundred twenty-one thousand, eight hundred thirty-five

   Difficulty: Hard

1. The expanded form of the number, 2,030,296 is ____.

   A. (2 x 1,000,000) + (3 x 10,000) + (2 x 1,000) + (9 x 10) + (6 x 1)

   B. (2 x 1,000,000) + (0 x 100,000) + (3 x 10,000) + (0 x 1,000) + (2 x 100) + (9 x 10) + (6 x 1)

   C. (2 x 1,000,000) + (0 x 100,000) + (3 x 100,000) + (0 x 1,000) + (2 x 100) + (9 x 10) + (6 x 1)

   D. (2 x 10,000,000) + (0 x 100,000) + (3 x 10,000) + (0 x 1,000) + (2 x 100) + (9 x 10) + (6 x 1)

   Difficulty: Hard

2. The mystery number has ...

   A 2 in the Hundred Thousands place.
   An 8 in the Tens place.
   A 5 in the Millions place.
   A 4 in the Ten Thousands place.
   A 3 in the Thousands place.
   A 6 in the Hundreds place.
   A 2 in the Ones place.

   What is the mystery number?

   E. 5,243,682
   F. 5,243,680
   G. 5,043,682
   H. 5,243,628

   Difficulty: Hard

3. The mystery number has ...

   A 7 in the Ten Thousands place.
   A 3 in the Thousands place.
   A 6 in the Hundreds place.

   What is the mystery number?

   A. 730,670   C. 73,670
   B. 703,670   D. 7,367

   Difficulty: Hard

4. The mystery number has ...

   A 2 in the Tens place.
   A 4 in the Thousands place.
   A 3 in the Ones place.
   A 1 in the Hundreds place.
   A 1 in the Millions place.
   A 1 in the Hundred Thousands place.

   What is the mystery number?

   E. 1,214,123   G. 1,004,123
   F. 1,104,123   H. 1,400,123

   Difficulty: Hard

5. What is the correct word name of the number, 9,943,675?

A. nine million, nine hundred forty thousand, six hundred seventy-five

B. nine million, nine hundred forty-three thousand, six hundred five

C. nine million, forty-three thousand, six hundred seventy-five

D. nine million, nine hundred forty-three thousand, six hundred seventy-five

Difficulty: Hard

6. What is the correct word name of the number, 675?

E. Six Hundred Seventy
F. Six Hundred Seventy - Five
G. Six Hundred Five
H. Six Hundred Fifty - Seven

Difficulty: Easy

7. What is the standard form of the number, seventy-two thousand, eight hundred seventy-eight?

A. 702,878   **C.** 7,878
B. 72,878   **D.** 72,870

Difficulty: Moderate

8. The mystery number has …

A **5** in the Hundred Thousands place.
A **2** in the Tens place.
A **7** in the Thousands place.
A **5** in the Hundreds place.
A **3** in the Millions place.

What is the mystery number?

E. 3,507,520   **G.** 3,705,520
F. 3,507,502   **H.** 3,507,250

Difficulty: Hard

1. The standard form of the number, One Million, Seven Hundred Thirty - Two Thousand, Four Hundred Fifty - Six, is ____.

   A. 1,732,546
   C. 1,732,456
   B. 1,723,456
   D. 1,743,256

   Difficulty: Hard

2. What is the word form of the standard number, 1,897?

   A. One Thousand, Eight Hundred Ninety
   B. One Thousand, Eight Hundred Seventy - Seven
   C. One Thousand, Seven Hundred Ninety - Seven
   D. One Thousand, Eight Hundred Ninety - Seven

   Difficulty: Moderate

3. What is the standard form of the number, $(9 \times 1,000,000)$ + $(3 \times 100,000)$ + $(9 \times 10,000)$ + $(9 \times 1,000)$ + (9×100) + (9×10) + (6×1)?

   A. 9,399,996
   C. 9,399,969
   B. 9,399,990
   D. 9,369,997

   Difficulty: Hard

4. What is the expanded form of the number, 3,407,051?

   E. $(3 \times 1,000,000)$ + $(4 \times 1,100,000)$ + $(7 \times 1,000)$ + (5×10) + (1×1)
   F. $(3 \times 1,000,000)$ + $(7 \times 100,000)$ + $(0 \times 10,000)$ + $(4 \times 1,000)$ + (0×100) + (5×10) + (1×1)
   G. $(3 \times 1,000,000)$ + $(4 \times 100,000)$ + (7×100) + (5×10) + (5×1)
   H. $(3 \times 1,000,000)$ + $(4 \times 100,000)$ + $(0 \times 10,000)$ + $(7 \times 1,000)$ + (0×100) + (5×10) + (1×1)

   Difficulty: Hard

5. What is the expanded form of the number, 9,568?

   A. $9 \times 1,000 + 6 \times 100 + 5 \times 10 + 8 \times 1$
   B. $9 \times 1,000 + 5 \times 100 + 8 \times 10 + 6 \times 1$
   C. $5 \times 1,000 + 9 \times 100 + 6 \times 10 + 8 \times 1$
   D. $9 \times 1,000 + 5 \times 100 + 6 \times 10 + 8 \times 1$

   Difficulty: Easy

6. Which of the following numbers is in the ten thousands place in 345,783?

   E. 3
   G. 5
   F. 4
   H. 7

   Difficulty: Moderate

7. Which of the following numbers is in the hundred millions place in the number, 4,839,902,126?

A. 4   C. 3
B. 8   D. 9

Difficulty: Moderate

8. Which of the following numbers is in the thousands place in the number, 239,150,876?

E. 5   G. 1
F. 2   H. 0

Difficulty: Moderate

9. Which of the following is the standard form of the number one million seventy-two?

A. 1,720,000   C. 1,000,720
B. 1,000,072   D. 1,072,000

Difficulty: Hard

10. Which of the following is the standard form of the number, one hundred two thousand, three hundred nine?

E. 102,309   G. 102,390
F. 103,209   H. 120,309

Difficulty: Hard

11. Which of the following is the expanded word form of the number 500,100,160?

A. five million, 1 hundred thousand, one hundred sixty
B. five hundred million, 1 hundred thousand, sixty
C. five hundred million, 1 hundred thousand, one hundred sixty
D. five hundred million, 1 ten thousand, one hundred sixty

Difficulty: Hard

12. What is the correct expanded form of the number, 9,485,342?

E. (9 x 1,000,000) + (4 x 100,000) + (8 x 10,000) + (3 x 1,000) + (5 x 100) + (4 x 10) + (2 x 1)

F. (9 x 1,000,000) + (8 x 100,000) + (4 x 10,000) + (5 x 1,000) + (3 x 100) + (4 x 10) + (2 x 1)

G. (9 x 1,000,000) + (4 x 100,000) + (8 x 10,000) + (5 x 1,000) + (3 x 100) + (4 x 10) + (2 x 1)

H. (9 x 1,000,000) + (4 x 100,000) + (8 x 10,000) + (4 x 1,000) + (3 x 100) + (5 x 10) + (2 x 1)

Difficulty: Hard

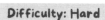

1. 56 is 7 times as many as _____.

   A. 6   C. 8
   B. 7   D. 9

   Difficulty: Easy

2. 10 is _____ times as many as 5.

   E. 2   G. 4
   F. 3   H. 5

   Difficulty: Easy

3. 12 is 4 times as many as _____.

   A. 2   C. 4
   B. 3   D. 5

   Difficulty: Easy

4. 72 is _____ times as many as 8.

   E. 7   G. 9
   F. 8   H. 6

   Difficulty: Easy

5. 9 times as many as 2 is _____.

   A. 12   C. 16
   B. 14   D. 18

   Difficulty: Easy

6. Determine which choice best represents the equation: 32 is 8 times as many as 4.

   E. $8 \times 8 = 32$ G. $4 \times 8 = 32$
   F. $8 + 4 = 32$ H. $8 + 8 = 32$

   Difficulty: Moderate

7. Determine which choice best represents the equation: 70 is 10 times as many as 7.

   A. $70 = 10 \times 10$
   B. $10 + 7 = 70$
   C. $7 \times 10 = 70$
   D. $70 = 7 + 10$

   Difficulty: Moderate

8. Determine which choice best represents the equation: 42 is 7 times as many as 6.

   E. $42 = 6 + 6$ G. $7 \times 6 = 42$
   F. $7 + 6 = 42$ H. $42 = 7 \times 7$

   Difficulty: Moderate

9. Determine which choice best represents the equation: 56 is 8 times as many as 7.

   A. $7 \times 7 = 56$ C. $8 + 8 = 56$
   B. $7 \times 8 = 56$ D. $56 = 7 + 7$

   Difficulty: Moderate

10. Determine which choice best represents the equation: 15 is 5 times as many as 3.

E. $3 + 5 = 15$ **G.** $5 \times 5 = 15$

F. $15 = 3 \times 5$ **H.** $3 \times 3 = 15$

Difficulty: Moderate

11. A flower shop has thirty-six tulips and six irises. How many times more tulips did they have than irises?

A. 6   **C.** 8

B. 7   **D.** 9

Difficulty: Moderate

12. A restaurant sold three times as many pizzas as they sold subs. If they sold seven subs, how many pizzas did they sell?

E. 5   **G.** 14

F. 7   **H.** 21

Difficulty: Moderate

13. The table below shows the number of books Lindsay read the first 3 months of school.

Month	Books Read
1	12
2	11
3	9

If Brandon read 3 times as many books as Lindsay, how many more books did Brandon read?

A. 32   **C.** 96

B. 64   **D.** 128

Difficulty: Hard

14. $248.92 \times 10^4 = $ ____.

E. 24,892   **G.** 489,200

F. 248,920   **H.** 2,489,200

Difficulty: Hard

15. $4.7 \div 10^3 = $ ____.

A. 0.0047   **C.** 0.47

B. 0.047   **D.** 47

Difficulty: Hard

1. $884.4 \div 10^2 = $ _____

   A. 8.0844   C. 8.844

   B. 18.844   D. .8844

   Difficulty: Hard

2. If $4 \times 9 = 36$, then $0.04 \times 0.009 = $

   _____

   E. 0.00036   G. 0.036

   F. 0.36   H. 0.0036

   Difficulty: Hard

3. If $6 \times 2 = 12$, then $0.06 \times 0.02 = $

   ____

   A. 0.0012   C. 0.12

   B. 0.012   D. 1.2

   Difficulty: Hard

4. $8 \times 10^3 = $ _____

   E. 80   G. 8,000

   F. 800   H. 80,000

   Difficulty: Moderate

5. $95 \times 10^4 = $ _____

   A. 950,000   C. 9,500

   B. 95,000   D. 950

   Difficulty: Moderate

6. $19 \times$ _____ $= 760$

   E. 40   G. 25

   F. 30   H. 45

   Difficulty: Moderate

7. $582 \times 75 = $ _____

   A. 4,365   C. 43,650

   B. 43,065   D. 436

   Difficulty: Moderate

8. $725 \times 16 = $ _____

   E. 11,610   G. 11,600

   F. 11,620   H. 11,650

   Difficulty: Moderate

9. $659 \times 56 = $ _____

   A. 3,694   C. 360,904

   B. 36,904   D. 36,909

   Difficulty: Hard

10. $287 \times 65 = $ _____

    E. 18,655   G. 1,865

    F. 1,655   H. 18,650

    Difficulty: Hard

11.

$$\begin{array}{r} 453 \\ \times\ 94 \\ \hline \end{array}$$

A. 1,812   C. 42,570

B. 40,770   D. 42,582

Difficult: Hard

12.

$$\begin{array}{r} 627 \\ \times\ 75 \\ \hline \end{array}$$

E. 47,520   G. 4,725

F. 475   H. 47,025

Difficult: Hard

13.

$$\begin{array}{r} 508 \\ \times\ 93 \\ \hline \end{array}$$

A. 47,244   C. 4,244

B. 4,244   D. 47,240

Difficulty: Hard

14. 330 × 71 = _____

E. 2,343   G. 23,430

F. 2,330   H. 23,435

Difficulty: Hard

15. 593 × 71 = _____

A. 4,213   C. 41,203

B. 42,130   D. 42,103

Difficulty: Hard

16. 9,315 × 92 = _____

E. 856,982   G. 85,698

F. 856,980   H. 8,569

Difficulty: Hard

17.

$$\begin{array}{r} 9,484 \\ \times\ 40 \\ \hline \end{array}$$

A. 379,360   C. 37,360

B. 3,760   D. 379,340

Difficulty: Hard

1. $338 \times 776 =$ _____

   E. 262,288   G. 2,288
   F. 26,288   H. 262,280

   Difficulty: Hard

2. $854 \times 533 =$ _____

   A. 45,182   C. 455,180
   B. 450,182   D. 455,182

   Difficulty: Hard

3. $984 \times 249 =$ _____

   E. 245,016   G. 24,516
   F. 24,016   H. 245,010

   Difficulty: Hard

4. $74 \times 11 =$ _____

   A. 810   C. 812
   B. 811   D. 814

   Difficulty: Moderate

5. $54 \times 91 =$ _____

   E. 4,910   G. 4,914
   F. 4,912   H. 4,941

   Difficulty: Moderate

6. $55 \times 81 =$ _____

   A. 455   C. 4,450
   B. 4,455   D. 4,405

   Difficulty: Moderate

7. $2,965 \times 542 =$ _____

   E. 1,607,030   G. 607,030
   F. 1,607   H. 1,607,300

   Difficulty: Hard

8. $2010 \times 46 =$ _____

   A. 9,552   C. 92,460
   B. 92,550   D. 92,052

   Difficulty: Hard

9. $24 \times 24 =$ _____

   E. 1,576   G. 5,176
   F. 576   H. 5,076

   Difficulty: Moderate

10. $3 \times 27 =$ _____

    A. 18   C. 810
    B. 180   D. 81

    Difficulty: Easy

11. 211 × 100 = _____

- **E.** 200
- **F.** 2,110
- **G.** 21,110
- **H.** 21,100

Difficulty: Moderate

12. 125 × 25 = _____

- **A.** 3,125
- **B.** 3,120
- **C.** 3,122
- **D.** 3,152

Difficulty: Moderate

13. 976 × 444 = _____

- **E.** 433,340
- **F.** 433,314
- **G.** 433,304
- **H.** 433,344

Difficulty: Hard

14. 661 × 5 = _____

- **A.** 3,035
- **B.** 3,350
- **C.** 3,305
- **D.** 3,300

Difficulty: Easy

15. 5,763 × 42 = _____

- **E.** 242,046
- **F.** 242,556
- **G.** 242,050
- **H.** 242,006

Difficulty: Moderate

16. 90 × 40 = _____

- **A.** 3,605
- **B.** 3,610
- **C.** 3,600
- **D.** 360

Difficulty: Moderate

17. 879 × 21 = _____

- **E.** 18,450
- **F.** 18,459
- **G.** 18,495
- **H.** 18,549

Difficulty: Moderate

18. 6,309 × 602 = _____

- **A.** 3,798,018
- **B.** 3,798,818
- **C.** 3,798,012
- **D.** 3,798,010

Difficulty: Hard

1. 165 ÷ 5 = _____

   A. 35   C. 30
   B. 33   D. 25

   Difficulty: Easy

2. 236 ÷ 4 = _____

   E. 58   G. 56
   F. 54   H. 59

   Difficulty: Easy

3. 448 ÷ 8 = _____

   A. 56   C. 65
   B. 45   D. 55

   Difficulty: Easy

4. 304 ÷ 8 = _____

   E. 36   G. 38
   F. 34   H. 32

   Difficulty: Easy

5. 162 ÷ 3 = _____

   A. 50   C. 56
   B. 54   D. 52

   Difficulty: Easy

6. 480 ÷ 6 = _____

   E. 80   G. 40
   F. 60   H. 30

   Difficulty: Easy

7. 427 ÷ 7 = _____

   A. 60   C. 62
   B. 71   D. 61

   Difficulty: Easy

8. 544 ÷ 8 = _____

   E. 66   G. 68
   F. 64   H. 62

   Difficulty: Easy

9. 765 ÷ 9 = _____

   A. 80   C. 83
   B. 85   D. 84

   Difficulty: Easy

10. 84 ÷ 4 = _____

   E. 21   G. 24
   F. 14   H. 22

   Difficulty: Easy

11. 429 ÷ 33 = _____

    A. 15   **C.** 13

    B. 16   **D.** 17

Difficulty: Moderate

12. 448 ÷ 28 = _____

    E. 14   **G.** 12

    F. 16   **H.** 22

Difficulty: Moderate

13. 5694 ÷ 78 = _____

    A. 71   **C.** 67

    B. 69   **D.** 73

Difficulty: Moderate

14. 2380 ÷ 85 = _____

    E. 26   **G.** 27

    F. 29   **H.** 28

Difficulty: Moderate

15. 12,328 ÷ 23 = _____

    A. 516   **C.** 536

    B. 506   **D.** 531

Difficulty: Moderate

16. 25,245 ÷ 99 = _____

    E. 255   **G.** 230

    F. 245   **H.** 265

Difficulty: Moderate

17. 15,012 ÷ 27 = _____

    A. 551   **C.** 558

    B. 556   **D.** 565

Difficulty: Moderate

18. 66,728 ÷ 76 = _____

    E. 876   **G.** 887

    F. 874   **H.** 878

Difficulty: Moderate

1. 4480 ÷ 20 = _____

A. 220   C. 222
B. 224   D. 228

Difficulty: Moderate

2. 6460 ÷ 38 = _____

E. 50   G. 170
F. 160   H. 180

Difficulty: Moderate

3. 7224 ÷ 56 = _____

A. 127   C. 121
B. 123   D. 129

Difficulty: Moderate

4. 4465 ÷ 47 = _____

E. 105   G. 85
F. 97   H. 95

Difficulty: Moderate

5. 1764 ÷ 18 = _____

A. 109   C. 98
B. 88   D. 108

Difficulty:

6. 2244 ÷ 66 = _____

E. 34   G. 43
F. 36   H. 42

Difficulty: Moderate

7. 9266 ÷ 41 = _____

A. 220   C. 228
B. 231   D. 226

Difficulty: Moderate

8. 544 ÷ 8 = _____

E. 68   G. 58
F. 48   H. 46

Difficulty: Moderate

9. 730 ÷ 6 = _____

A. 122 R 2   C. 120 R 4
B. 120 R 2   D. 121 R 4

Difficulty: Moderate

10. 452 ÷ 4 = _____

E. 112   G. 143
F. 113   H. 123

Difficulty: Moderate

11. 7108 ÷ 61 = _____

    A. 122 R 18   **C.** 116 R 32

    B. 118 R 24   **D.** 120 R 20

Difficulty: Moderate

12. 7108 ÷ 70 = _____

    E. 101 R 38   **G.** 110 R 38

    F. 138 R 1   **H.** 101 R 36

Difficulty: Moderate

13. 3783 ÷ 46 = _____

    A. 84 R 12   **C.** 82 R 11

    B. 82 R 12   **D.** 84 R 11

Difficulty: Moderate

14. 5864 ÷ 36 = _____

    E. 158 R 30   **G.** 160 R 30

    F. 161 R 32   **H.** 162 R 32

Difficulty: Moderate

15. 9,059 ÷ 47 = _____

    A. 182 R 35   **C.** 192 R 33

    B. 192 R 35   **D.** 194 R 35

Difficulty: Hard

16. 4,800 ÷ 20 = _____

    E. 120   **G.** 200

    F. 220   **H.** 240

Difficulty: Hard

17. 5,510 ÷ 56 = _____

    A. 98 R 22   **C.** 96 R 12

    B. 98 R 2   **D.** 94 R 24

Difficulty: Hard

18. 3,067 ÷ 21 = _____

    E. 146 R 11   **G.** 146 R 1

    F. 126 R 1   **H.** 146 R 10

Difficulty: Hard

1. $6{,}095 \div 86 =$ _____

   A. 70 R 70   **C.** 72 R 75
   B. 70 R 75   **D.** 70 R 65

   Difficulty: Hard

2. $5{,}288 \div 41 =$ _____

   E. 128 R 40   **G.** 128 R 44
   F. 126 R 40   **H.** 118 R 40

   Difficulty: Hard

3. $8{,}260 \div 236 =$ _____

   A. 33   **C.** 35
   B. 31   **D.** 43

   Difficulty: Hard

4. $5{,}769 \div 64 =$ _____

   E. 90 R 11   **G.** 90 R 19
   F. 80 R 9   **H.** 90 R 9

   Difficulty: Hard

5. $9{,}299 \div 47 =$ _____

   A. 197 R 20   **C.** 195 R 40
   B. 197 R 40   **D.** 193 R 42

   Difficulty: Hard

6. $9{,}114 \div 69 =$ _____

   E. 122 R 6   **G.** 132 R 6
   F. 112 R 6   **H.** 130 R 6

   Difficulty: Hard

7. $2{,}093 \div 98 =$ _____

   A. 21 R 35   **C.** 20 R 35
   B. 21 R 33   **D.** 23 R 35

   Difficulty: Hard

8. $7{,}238 \div 84 =$ _____

   E. 84 R 12   **G.** 86 R 12
   F. 82 R 14   **H.** 86 R 14

   Difficulty: Hard

9. $2{,}008 \div 76 =$ _____

   A. 26 R 28   **C.** 22 R 32
   B. 26 R 32   **D.** 24 R 32

   Difficulty: Hard

10. $5{,}688 \div 88 =$ _____

    E. 66 R 56   **G.** 62 R 58
    F. 64 R 58   **H.** 64 R 56

    Difficulty: Hard

11. 9,900 ÷ 75 = _____

   A. 132   C. 128
   B. 130   D. 131

   Difficulty: Hard

12. 2,233 ÷ 77 = _____

   E. 27   G. 25
   F. 29   H. 31

   Difficulty: Hard

13. 9,246 ÷ 41 = _____

   A. 225 R 21   C. 215 R 21
   B. 225 R 12   D. 205 R 21

   Difficulty: Hard

14. 54,000 ÷ 9,000 = _____

   E. 4   G. 6
   F. 5   H. 7

   Difficulty: Moderate

1. Is 88 a prime or composite number?

   A. prime   **B.** composite

   Difficulty: Easy

2. Is 14 a prime or composite number?

   A. prime   **B.** composite

   Difficulty: Easy

3. Is 71 a prime or composite number?

   A. prime   **B.** composite

   Difficulty: Moderate

4. Is 84 a prime or composite number?

   A. prime   **B.** composite

   Difficulty: Easy

5. Is 61 a prime or composite number?

   A. prime   **B.** composite

   Difficulty: Moderate

6. Is 35 a prime or composite number?

   A. prime   **B.** composite

   Difficulty: Easy

7. Is 30 a prime or composite number?

   A. prime   **B.** composite

   Difficulty: Easy

8. Is 43 a prime or composite number?

   A. prime   **B.** composite

   Difficulty: Moderate

9. Is 74 a prime or composite number?

   A. prime   **B.** composite

   Difficulty: Easy

10. Is 13 a prime or composite number?

    A. prime   **B.** composite

    Difficulty: Easy

11. Is 85 a prime or composite number?

    A. prime   **B.** composite

    Difficulty: Easy

12. Is 81 a prime or composite number?

    A. prime   **B.** composite

    Difficulty: Moderate

13. Is 23 a prime or composite number?

A. prime   **B.** composite

Difficulty: Moderate

14. Is 11 a prime or composite number?

A. prime   **B.** composite

Difficulty: Moderate

15. Is 41 a prime or composite number?

A. prime   **B.** composite

Difficulty: Moderate

16. Is 91 a prime or composite number?

A. prime   **B.** composite

Difficulty: Moderate

17. Is 83 a prime or composite number?

A. prime   **B.** composite

Difficulty: Moderate

18. Is 37 a prime or composite number?

A. prime   **B.** composite

Difficulty: Moderate

19. Is 20 a prime or composite number?

A. prime   **B.** composite

Difficulty: Easy

20. Is 3 a prime or composite number?

A. prime   **B.** composite

Difficulty: Easy

1. Is 17 a prime or composite number?

   A. prime   **B.** composite

   Difficulty: Easy

2. Is 81 a prime or composite number?

   A. prime   **B.** composite

   Difficulty: Moderate

3. Is 53 a prime or composite number?

   A. prime   **B.** composite

   Difficulty: Moderate

4. Is 65 a prime or composite number?

   A. prime   **B.** composite

   Difficulty: Easy

5. Is 56 a prime or composite number?

   A. prime   **B.** composite

   Difficulty: Easy

6. Is 23 a prime or composite number?

   A. prime   **B.** composite

   Difficulty: Moderate

7. Is 59 a prime or composite number?

   A. prime   **B.** composite

   Difficulty: Moderate

8. Is 13 a prime or composite number?

   A. prime   **B.** composite

   Difficulty: Easy

9. Is 41 a prime or composite number?

   A. prime   **B.** composite

   Difficulty: Moderate

10. Is 88 a prime or composite number?

    A. prime   **B.** composite

    Difficulty: Easy

11. Is 27 a prime or composite number?

    A. prime   **B.** composite

    Difficulty: Easy

12. Is 68 a prime or composite number?

    A. prime   **B.** composite

    Difficulty: Easy

13. Is 66 a prime or composite number?

A. prime   **B.** composite

Difficulty: Easy

14. Is 72 a prime or composite number?

A. prime   **B.** composite

Difficulty: Easy

15. Is 67 a prime or composite number?

A. prime   **B.** composite

Difficulty: Moderate

16. Is 100 a prime or composite number?

A. prime   **B.** composite

Difficulty: Easy

17. Is 22 a prime or composite number?

A. prime   **B.** composite

Difficulty: Easy

18. Is 73 a prime or composite number?

A. prime   **B.** composite

Difficulty: Moderate

19. Is 7 a prime or composite number?

A. prime   **B.** composite

Difficulty: Easy

20. Is 83 a prime or composite number?

A. prime   **B.** composite

Difficulty: Moderate

1. Is 77 a prime or composite number?

   A. prime   **B.** composite

   Difficulty: Moderate

2. Is 89 a prime or composite number?

   A. prime   **B.** composite

   Difficulty: Moderate

3. Is 19 a prime or composite number?

   A. prime   **B.** composite

   Difficulty: Moderate

4. Is 31 a prime or composite number?

   A. prime   **B.** composite

   Difficulty: Moderate

5. Is 42 a prime or composite number?

   A. prime   **B.** composite

   Difficulty: Moderate

6. Is 63 a prime or composite number?

   A. prime   **B.** composite

   Difficulty: Moderate

7. Is 51 a prime or composite number?

   A. prime   **B.** composite

   Difficulty: Moderate

8. Is 57 a prime or composite number?

   A. prime   **B.** composite

   Difficulty: Moderate

9. Is 2 a prime or composite number?

   A. prime   **B.** composite

   Difficulty: Easy

10. Is 91 a prime or composite number?

   A. prime   **B.** composite

   Difficulty: Moderate

1. What are all the factors of **25**?

    A. 1, 25
    B. 1, 3, 5, 25
    C. 1, 5, 25
    D. 1, 3, 25

Difficulty: Easy

2. What are all the factors of **51**?

    E. 1, 3, 5, 17, 51
    F. 1, 5, 17, 51
    G. 1, 3, 5, 51
    H. 1, 3, 17, 51

Difficulty: Easy

3. What are all the factors of **34**?

    A. 1, 2, 8, 17, 34
    B. 1, 2, 12, 17, 34
    C. 1, 2, 3, 17, 34
    D. 1, 2, 17, 34

Difficulty: Easy

4. What are all the factors of **117**?

    E. 1, 3, 9, 13, 33, 39, 117
    F. 1, 3, 9, 13, 23, 39, 117
    G. 1, 3, 9, 13, 15, 39, 117
    H. 1, 3, 9, 13, 39, 117

Difficulty: Moderate

5. What are all the factors of **94**?

    A. 1 ,2, 47, 94
    B. 1 ,2, 4, 47, 94
    C. 1 ,2, 8, 12, 47, 94
    D. 1 ,2, 24, 47, 94

Difficulty: Moderate

6. What are all the factors of **76**?

    E. 1, 2, 19, 38, 76
    F. 1, 2, 4, 19, 38, 76
    G. 1, 2, 4, 6, 19, 38, 76
    H. 1, 4, 19, 38, 76

Difficulty: Moderate

7. What are all the factors of **142**?

    A. 1, 2, 21, 71, 142
    B. 1, 2, 71, 142
    C. 1, 2, 3, 21, 71, 142
    D. 1, 2, 33, 71, 142

Difficulty: Moderate

8. What are all the factors of **106**?

    E. 1, 2, 4, 12, 53, 106
    F. 1, 2, 3, 12, 53, 106
    G. 1, 2, q, 16, 53, 106
    H. 1, 2, 53, 106

Difficulty: Moderate

9. What are all the factors of 139?

A. 1, 139
B. 1, 13, 139
C. 1, 3, 33, 139
D. 1, 13, 17, 139

Difficulty: Easy

10. What are all the factors of 130?

E. 1, 2, 3, 5, 10, 13, 26, 65, 130
F. 1, 2, 5, 10, 13, 15, 26, 65, 130
G. 1, 2, 5, 10, 13, 26, 65, 130
H. 1, 2, 5, 10, 13, 17, 26, 65, 130

Difficulty: Moderate

11. What are all the factors of 95?

A. 1, 5, 15, 19, 95
B. 1, 5, 7, 15, 19, 95
C. 1, 5, 19, 95
D. 1, 5, 19, 25, 95

Difficulty: Moderate

12. What are all the factors of 10?

E. 1, 2, 5, 10
F. 1, 5, 10
G. 1, 2, 3, 5, 10
H. 1, 2, 5, 6, 10

Difficulty: Moderate

13. What are all the factors of 16?

A. 1, 2, 4, 6, 8, 16
B. 1, 2, 4, 8, 16
C. 1, 2, 4, 8, 12, 16
D. 1, 2, 3, 4, 8, 16

Difficulty: Moderate

14. What are all the factors of 124?

E. 1, 2, 4, 6, 31, 62, 124
F. 1, 2, 4, 12, 31, 62, 124
G. 1, 2, 4, 12, 14, , 62, 124
H. 1, 2, 4, 31, 62, 124

Difficulty: Moderate

15. What are all the factors of 46?

A. 1, 2, 4, 23, 46
B. 1, 2, 23, 46
C. 1, 2, 4, 6, 23, 46
D. 1, 2, 4, 12, 23, 46

Difficulty: Moderate

16. What are all the factors of 126?

E. 1, 2, 3, 6, 9, 14, 18, 21, 42, 63, 126
F. 1, 2, 3, 6, 7, 9, 14, 21, 42, 63, 126
G. 1, 2, 3, 6, 7, 9, 14, 18, 21, 42, 126
H. 1, 2, 3, 6, 7, 9, 14, 18, 21, 42, 63, 126

Difficulty: Hard

1. What are all the factors of 44?

    A. 1, 2, 4, 11, 12, 22, 44
    B. 1, 2, 4, 11, 22, 44
    C. 1, 2, 3, 4, 11, 22, 44
    D. 1, 2, 4, 11, 16, 22, 44

                  Difficulty: Moderate

2. What are all the factors of 114?

    E. 1, 2, 3, 6, 19, 38, 57, 114
    F. 1, 2, 3, 6, 19, 38, 114
    G. 1, 2, 3, 6, 19, 57, 114
    H. 1, 2, 3, 6, 19, 38, 47, 114

                  Difficulty: Moderate

3. What are all the factors of 81?

    A. 1, 3, 9, 11, 27, 81
    B. 1, 3, 9, 13, 27, 81
    C. 1, 3, 9, 27, 81
    D. 1, 9, 27, 81

                  Difficulty: Moderate

4. What are all the factors of 138?

    E. 1, 2, 3, 6, 23, 46, 138
    F. 1, 2, 3, 6, 23, 46, 69, 138
    G. 1, 2, 3, 6, 23, 33, 46, 69, 138
    H. 1, 2, 3, 6, 12, 23, 46, 69, 138

                  Difficulty: Hard

5. What is the greatest common factor of 60 and 24?

    A. 12   **C.** 8
    B. 10   **D.** 6

                  Difficulty: Moderate

6. What is the greatest common factor of 12 and 24?

    E. 6   **G.** 10
    F. 9   **H.** 12

                  Difficulty: Easy

7. What is the greatest common factor of 10 and 3?

    A. 3   **C.** 1
    B. 10   **D.** 0

                  Difficulty: Easy

8. What is the greatest common factor of 12 and 5?

    E. 12   **G.** 1
    F. 5   **H.** 0

                  Difficulty: Easy

9. What is the greatest common factor of 6 and 30?

A. 2
B. 4
C. 30
D. 6

Difficulty: Moderate

10. What is the greatest common factor of 40 and 15?

E. 40
F. 15
G. 3
H. 5

Difficulty: Moderate

11. What is the greatest common factor of 20 and 15?

A. 12
B. 24
C. 60
D. 5

Difficulty: Easy

12. What is the greatest common factor of 8 and 30?

E. 8
F. 30
G. 2
H. 1

Difficulty: Moderate

13. What is the greatest common factor of 2 and 3?

A. 0
B. 1
C. 2
D. 6

Difficulty: Easy

1. Which number is a factor of 18, but not a multiple of **6**?

   E. 12   **G.** 9

   F. 8   **H.** 10

Difficulty: Moderate

2. Which number is a factor of 24, but not a multiple of 12?

   A. 7   **C.** 5

   B. 9   **D.** 8

Difficulty: Hard

3. Which number is a factor of 10, but not a multiple of 5?

   E. 2   **G.** 6

   F. 8   **H.** 4

Difficulty: Hard

4. Which number is a factor of 16, but not a multiple of 8?

   A. 10   **C.** 12

   B. 6   **D.** 4

Difficulty: Hard

5. Which number is a factor of 24, but not a multiple of 2?

   E. 6   **G.** 8

   F. 3   **H.** 4

Difficulty: Hard

6. Which number is a factor of 12, but not a multiple of 6?

   A. 9   **C.** 4

   B. 10   **D.** 8

Difficulty: Hard

7. Which number is a factor of 14, but not a multiple of 2?

   E. 3   **G.** 5

   F. 7   **H.** 4

Difficulty: Hard

8. Which number is a factor of 22, but not a multiple of 11?

   A. 5   **C.** 2

   B. 6   **D.** 4

Difficulty: Hard

9. Which number is a factor of 8, but not a multiple of 4?

   E. 3   G. 2

   F. 5   H. 6

   Difficulty: Hard

10. Which number is a factor of 10, but not a multiple of 2?

   A. 6   C. 4

   B. 8   D. 5

   Difficulty: Hard

11. Which number is a factor of 18, but not a multiple of 9?

   E. 8   G. 5

   F. 4   H. 6

   Difficulty: Hard

12. Which number is a factor of 20, but not a multiple of 4?

   A. 6   C. 8

   B. 5   D. 12

   Difficulty: Hard

1. Which choice is not a factor of 92?

   E. 46 G. 10
   F. 2   H. 4

   Difficulty: Easy

2. Which choice is not a factor of 84?

   A. 3 C. 14
   B. 16 D. 2

   Difficulty: Easy

3. Which choice is not a factor of 96?

   E. 32 G. 5
   F. 48 H. 24

   Difficulty: Easy

4. Which choice is not a factor of 28?

   A. 2 C. 4
   B. 18 D. 14

   Difficulty: Easy

5. Which choice is not a factor of 45?

   E. 15 G. 3
   F. 20 H. 5

   Difficulty: Easy

6. Which choice is not a factor of 42?

   A. 2 C. 17
   B. 21 D. 6

   Difficulty: Easy

7. Which choice is a factor of 40?

   E. 3 G. 12
   F. 11 H. 5

   Difficulty: Easy

8. Which choice is a factor of 76?

   A. 9 C. 38
   B. 3 D. 14

   Difficulty: Easy

9. Which choice is a factor of 50?

   E. 10 G. 9
   F. 15 H. 6

   Difficulty: Easy

1. Which of the following shows 31,002 rounded to the nearest thousand?

   A. 31,005
   B. 31,000
   C. 32,000
   D. 30,000

   Difficulty: Moderate

2. Which of the following shows 415,690 rounded to the nearest hundred thousand?____.

   E. 400,000
   F. 420,000
   G. 425,000
   H. 420,700

   Difficulty: Hard

3. Which of the following shows 269 rounded to the nearest ten?

   A. 280
   B. 300
   C. 200
   D. 270

   Difficulty: Easy

4. Which of the following shows 105 rounded to the nearest hundred?

   E. 100
   F. 110
   G. 150
   H. 200

   Difficulty: Easy

5. Which of the following shows 7,783 rounded to the nearest hundred?

   A. 7,700
   B. 7,500
   C. 7,800
   D. 7,000

   Difficulty: Moderate

6. Which of the following shows 1,247 rounded to the nearest ten?

   E. 1,200
   F. 1,250
   G. 1,300
   H. 1,275

   Difficulty: Moderate

7. Which of the following shows 79,175 rounded to the nearest ten thousand?

   A. 90,000
   B. 75,000
   C. 85,000
   D. 80,000

   Difficulty: Moderate

8. Which of the following shows 4,022 rounded to the nearest thousand?

   E. 4,000
   F. 4,100
   G. 4,200
   H. 3,900

   Difficulty: Moderate

9. Which of the following shows **622,234** rounded to the nearest ten?

A. 622,200   C. 622,000

B. 622,230   D. 620,000

Difficulty: Easy

10. Which of the following shows **825** rounded to the nearest hundred?

E. 810   G. 850

F. 820   H. 800

Difficulty: Easy

11. Which of the following shows **682,769** rounded to the nearest hundred?

A. 682,000   C. 682,800

B. 682,870   D. 682,700

Difficult: Hard

12. Which of the following shows **57,909** rounded to the nearest thousand?

E. 58,000   G. 57,000

F. 57,900   H. 57,910

Difficult: Hard

13. Which of the following shows **31,191** rounded to the nearest thousand?

A. 31,200   C. 31,000

B. 31,190   D. 31,100

Difficulty: Hard

14. Which of the following shows **292,147** rounded to the nearest hundred thousand?

E. 290,000   G. 310,000

F. 292,000   H. 300,000

Difficulty: Hard

15. Which of the following shows **6,830** rounded to the nearest thousand?

A. 7,000   C. 6,750

B. 6,800   D. 7,800

Difficulty: Moderate

1. Which of the following shows 58,111 rounded to the nearest ten?

A. 58,000   C. 58,110

B. 58,100   D. 57,900

Difficulty: Moderate

2. Which of the following shows 170 rounded to the nearest hundred?

E. 150   G. 100

F. 175   H. 200

Difficulty: Easy

3. Which of the following shows 9,959 rounded to the nearest thousand?

A. 10,000   C. 9,900

B. 9,000   D. 10,900

Difficulty: Moderate

4. Which of the following shows 146 rounded to the nearest ten?

E. 200   G. 100

F. 150   H. 175

Difficulty: Easy

5. Which of the following shows 244,844 rounded to the nearest hundred thousand?

A. 240,000   C. 250,000

B. 245,000   D. 200,000

Difficult: Hard

6. Which of the following shows 255.111 rounded to the nearest hundredth?

E. 255.11   G. 300

F. 255.1   H. 255

Difficult: Hard

7. Which of the following shows 64.530 rounded to the nearest hundredth?

A. 64.5   C. 64.53

B. 64.531   D. 64

Difficult: Hard

8. Which of the following shows 24.190 rounded to the nearest tenth?

E. 24.1   G. 24.19

F. 24.2   H. 24

Difficult: Hard

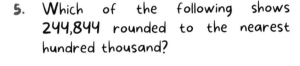

9. Which of the following shows 456.025 rounded to the nearest tenth?

   A. 456.02 **C.** 456.5

   B. 456.0 **D.** 457

   Difficult: Hard

10. Which of the following shows 68.152 rounded to the nearest hundredth?

    E. 68 **G.** 68.15

    F. 68.2 **H.** 68.152

    Difficult: Hard

11. Which of the following shows 5.77 rounded to the nearest tenth?

    - **A.** 5.8 **C.** 5.70

    B. 5.7 **D.** 5

    Difficulty: Moderate

12. Which of the following shows 366.66 rounded to the nearest tenth?

    E. 366 **G.** 366.7

    F. 366.67 **H.** 367

    Difficulty: Moderate

13. Which of the following shows 91.132 rounded to the nearest hundredth?

    A. 91 **C.** 91.1

    B. 91.13 **D.** 91.3

    Difficulty: Moderate

14. Which of the following shows 8.4 rounded to the nearest whole number?

    E. 8.4 **G.** 8

    F. 8.0 **H.** 8.1

    Difficulty: Easy

15. Which of the following shows 8.16 rounded to the nearest tenth?

    A. 8.2 **C.** 8.1

    B. 8 **D.** 8.02

    Difficulty: Easy

16. Which of the following shows 80.4 rounded to the nearest whole number?

    E. 80 **G.** 79

    F. 81 **H.** 85

    Difficulty: Easy

1. Which of the following shows 495.535 rounded to the nearest whole number?

   A. 495   **C.** 496

   B. 490   **D.** 500

   Difficulty: Moderate

2. Which of the following shows 6.5 rounded to the nearest whole number?

   E. 6   **G.** 7

   F. 5   **H.** 10

   Difficulty: Easy

3. Which of the following shows 6.692 rounded to the nearest hundredth?

   A. 6.7   **C.** 6.6

   B. 6   **D.** 6.69

   Difficulty: Moderate

4. Which of the following shows 66.36 rounded to the nearest tenth?

   E. 66   **G.** 66.3

   F. 66.4   **H.** 66.5

   Difficulty: Moderate

5. 36. Which of the following shows 8.751 rounded to the nearest hundredth?

   A. 8.75   **C.** 8.7

   B. 8.8   **D.** 8

   Difficulty: Moderate

6. Which of the following shows 15.124 rounded to the nearest whole number?

   E. 16   **G.** 15

   F. 15.1   **H.** 15.2

   Difficulty: Moderate

7. Which of the following shows 95.569 rounded to the nearest hundredth?

   A. 95.57   **C.** 95.5

   B. 95.6   **D.** 95.7

   Difficulty: Moderate

8. Which of the following shows 7.47 rounded to the nearest tenth?

   E. 7.5   **G.** 7.7

   F. 7   **H.** 7.6

   Difficulty: Moderate

9. Which of the following shows 947.036 rounded to the nearest whole number?

A. 947.136   **C.** 947.1

B. 947   **D.** 947.03

Difficulty: Hard

10. Which of the following shows 6.48 rounded to the nearest tenth?

E. 6.40   **G.** 6.5

F. 6.58   **H.** 6.49

Difficulty: Moderate

11. Which of the following shows 56.34 rounded to the nearest tenth?

A. 56.4   **C.** 56.40

B. 56.3   **D.** 56.2

Difficulty: Moderate

12. Which of the following shows 2.346 rounded to the nearest hundredth?

E. 2.34   **G.** 2.35

F. 2.3   **H.** 2.44

Difficulty: Hard

13. Which of the following shows 45.841 rounded to the nearest hundredth?

A. 45.85   **C.** 45.9

B. 45.84   **D.** 45.8

Difficulty: Moderate

14. Which of the following shows 23.385 rounded to the nearest hundredth?

E. 23.39   **G.** 23.40

F. 23.38   **H.** 23.48

Difficulty: Hard

15. Which of the following shows 6.8375 rounded to the nearest thousandth?

A. 6.837   **C.** 6.848

B. 6.838   **D.** 6.830

Difficulty: Hard

16. Which of the following shows 0.0046 rounded to the nearest thousandth?

E. 0.005   **G.** 0.004

F. 0.05   **H.** 0.047

Difficulty: Hard

1. $2\frac{1}{4} + 2\frac{2}{4} =$ _____

 A. 4

 B. $4\frac{1}{2}$

 C. $4\frac{3}{4}$

 D. $4\frac{1}{4}$

 Difficulty: Easy

2. $2\frac{2}{8} + 1\frac{5}{8} =$ _____

 E. $3\frac{7}{8}$

 F. $3\frac{5}{8}$

 G. $3\frac{1}{8}$

 H. $\frac{32}{8}$

 Difficulty: Easy

3. $1\frac{2}{4} + 1\frac{2}{4} =$ _____

 A. $2\frac{2}{4}$

 B. 2

 C. $2\frac{3}{4}$

 D. 3

 Difficulty: Easy

4. $3\frac{2}{3} + 2\frac{1}{3} =$ _____

 E. $5\frac{2}{3}$

 F. 6

 G. $5\frac{3}{4}$

 H. $6\frac{1}{3}$

 Difficulty: Easy

5. $2\frac{2}{4} + 3\frac{1}{4} =$ _____

 A. $5\frac{2}{4}$

 B. $5\frac{3}{4}$

 C. $6\frac{1}{4}$

 D. $5\frac{1}{3}$

 Difficulty: Easy

6. $3\frac{1}{4} + 1\frac{1}{4} =$ _____

 E. 4

 F. $2\frac{1}{4}$

 G. $4\frac{1}{4}$

 H. $4\frac{2}{4}$

 Difficulty: Easy

7. $3\frac{1}{5} + 3\frac{2}{5} =$ _____

 A. $5\frac{3}{5}$

 B. $6\frac{3}{5}$

 C. $6\frac{1}{5}$

 D. $5\frac{4}{5}$

 Difficulty: Easy

8. $1\frac{1}{3} + 2\frac{2}{3} =$ _____

 E. $3\frac{3}{4}$

 F. $4\frac{1}{4}$

 G. 4

 H. $4\frac{2}{4}$

 Difficulty: Easy

9. $1\frac{1}{4} + 2\frac{3}{4} =$ _____

    A. 4 C. $4\frac{2}{4}$

    B. $4\frac{1}{4}$ D. $3\frac{3}{4}$

Difficulty: Easy

10. $3\frac{5}{8} + 2\frac{4}{8} =$ _____

    E. $5\frac{7}{8}$ G. $6\frac{2}{8}$

    F. $6\frac{1}{8}$ H. $5\frac{5}{8}$

Difficulty: Easy

11. $3\frac{2}{5} + 2\frac{4}{5} =$ _____

    A. 6 C. $5\frac{4}{5}$

    B. $6\frac{1}{5}$ D. $6\frac{3}{5}$

Difficulty: Easy

12. $3\frac{2}{6} + 1\frac{1}{6} =$ _____

    E. $4\frac{1}{6}$ G. $4\frac{2}{6}$

    F. 4 H. $4\frac{3}{6}$

Difficulty: Easy

13. $7\frac{4}{5} - 2\frac{1}{5} =$ _____

    A. $5\frac{1}{8}$ C. $5\frac{7}{8}$

    B. $5\frac{3}{5}$ D. 6

Difficulty: Easy

14. $6\frac{3}{6} - 3\frac{2}{6} =$ _____

    E. $3\frac{1}{6}$ G. $4\frac{3}{6}$

    F. $4\frac{1}{6}$ H. $1\frac{1}{6}$

Difficulty: Easy

15. $3\frac{4}{10} - 1\frac{8}{10} =$ _____

    A. $1\frac{2}{10}$ C. $1\frac{6}{10}$

    B. $2\frac{8}{10}$ D. $1\frac{7}{10}$

Difficulty: Easy

16. $3\frac{4}{12} - 1\frac{10}{12} =$ _____

    E. $1\frac{7}{12}$ G. $1\frac{6}{12}$

    F. $2\frac{1}{12}$ H. $1\frac{8}{12}$

Difficulty: Moderate

1. $7\frac{1}{3} - 5\frac{1}{3} = $ _____

   A. 3

   B. $2\frac{2}{3}$

   C. $1\frac{1}{3}$

   D. 2

   Difficulty: Easy

2. $6\frac{7}{10} - 4\frac{8}{10} = $ _____

   E. $2\frac{9}{10}$

   F. $1\frac{9}{10}$

   G. 2

   H. $1\frac{7}{10}$

   Difficulty: Moderate

3. $1\frac{5}{6} - 1\frac{2}{6} = $ _____

   A. 2

   B. $\frac{3}{6}$

   C. $1\frac{5}{6}$

   D. $2\frac{1}{6}$

   Difficulty: Moderate

4. $4\frac{2}{3} - 1\frac{2}{3} = $ _____

   E. 2

   F. $2\frac{2}{3}$

   G. $3\frac{1}{3}$

   H. 3

   Difficulty: Easy

5. Which two whole numbers does the fraction $4\frac{4}{5}$ lie between?

   A. 3 and 4

   B. 4 and 5

   C. 5 and 6

   D. 2 and 3

   Difficulty: Hard

6. Which two whole numbers does the fraction $8\frac{1}{6}$ lie between?

   E. 8 and 9

   F. 7 and 8

   G. 9 and 10

   H. 6 and 7

   Difficulty: Hard

7. Which two whole numbers does the fraction $\frac{18}{5}$ lie between?

   A. 1 and 2

   B. 18 and 19

   C. 4 and 5

   D. 3 and 4

   Difficulty: Hard

8. Which two whole numbers does the fraction $\frac{44}{5}$ lie between?

   E. 5 and 6

   F. 44 and 45

   G. 8 and 9

   H. 9 and 10

   Difficulty: Hard

9. Which two whole numbers does the fraction $\frac{74}{10}$ lies between?

  A. 8 and 9   **C.** 74 and 75

  B. 7 and 8   **D.** 9 and 10

                        Difficulty: Hard

10. $\frac{2}{3} - \frac{6}{10} = $ _____

  E. $\frac{1}{30}$ **G.** $\frac{5}{30}$

  F. $\frac{2}{30}$ **H.** $\frac{12}{30}$

                    Difficulty: Moderate

11. $\frac{4}{6} + \frac{1}{4} = $ _____

  A. $\frac{1}{12}$ **C.** $\frac{9}{12}$

  B. $\frac{7}{12}$ **D.** $\frac{11}{12}$

                    Difficulty: Moderate

12. $\frac{2}{4} + \frac{1}{2} = $ _____

  E. $\frac{3}{4}$ **G.** $\frac{4}{4}$

  F. $\frac{1}{8}$ **H.** $\frac{3}{8}$

                    Difficulty: Moderate

13. $\frac{5}{6} - \frac{2}{4} = $ _____

  A. $\frac{1}{24}$ **C.** $\frac{4}{12}$

  B. $\frac{7}{12}$ **D.** $\frac{11}{12}$

                    Difficulty: Moderate

14. $\frac{4}{6} + \frac{2}{5} = $ _____

  E. $\frac{29}{30}$ **G.** $\frac{11}{30}$

  F. $\frac{32}{30}$ **H.** $\frac{17}{30}$

                    Difficulty: Moderate

15. $\frac{2}{3} \times 7 = $ _____

  A. $\frac{11}{7}$ **C.** $\frac{15}{3}$

  B. $\frac{14}{3}$ **D.** $\frac{9}{9}$

                    Difficulty: Hard

16. $\frac{2}{3} \times 3 = $ _____

  E. $\frac{3}{3}$ **G.** $\frac{6}{3}$

  F. $\frac{1}{3}$ **H.** $\frac{5}{3}$

                    Difficulty: Hard

17. $\frac{1}{6} \times 9 =$ _____

   A. $\frac{9}{6}$ C. $\frac{6}{9}$

   B. $\frac{5}{6}$ D. $\frac{4}{9}$

   Difficulty: Hard

18. $\frac{3}{5} \times \frac{2}{3} =$ _____

   E. $\frac{2}{15}$ G. $\frac{4}{15}$

   F. $\frac{6}{15}$ H. $\frac{7}{15}$

   Difficulty: Hard

19. $5 \div \frac{1}{9} =$ _____

   A. 54   C. 40

   B. 45   D. 35

   Difficulty: Hard

20. $6 \div \frac{1}{4} =$ _____

   E. 18   G. 24

   F. 48   H. 36

   Difficulty: Hard

21. $6 \div \frac{2}{3} =$ _____

   A. 9   C. 12

   B. 5   D. 6

   Difficulty: Hard

22. $3 \div \frac{4}{5} =$ _____

   E. 12   G. $2\frac{3}{4}$

   F. $\frac{12}{15}$ H. $3\frac{3}{4}$

   Difficulty: Hard

23. Reduce $\frac{8}{28}$ to its simplest form.

   A. $\frac{2}{7}$ C. $\frac{1}{7}$

   B. $\frac{4}{14}$ D. 7

   Difficulty: Hard

24. Reduce $\frac{12}{50}$ to its simplest form.

   E. $\frac{3}{4}$ G. $\frac{6}{25}$

   F. $\frac{2}{25}$ H. $\frac{4}{12}$

   Difficulty: Hard

1. Reduce $\frac{18}{24}$ to its simplest form.

   A. $\frac{2}{3}$

   B. $\frac{3}{4}$

   C. $\frac{1}{3}$

   D. $\frac{1}{4}$

   Difficulty: Hard

2. Reduce $\frac{9}{54}$ to its simplest form.

   E. $\frac{1}{3}$

   F. $\frac{1}{4}$

   G. $\frac{1}{9}$

   H. $\frac{1}{6}$

   Difficulty: Hard

3. $4\frac{6}{10} =$ _____

   A. $\frac{56}{10}$

   B. $\frac{46}{10}$

   C. $\frac{32}{10}$

   D. $\frac{40}{10}$

   Difficulty: Hard

4. $7\frac{8}{9} =$ _____

   E. $\frac{71}{9}$

   F. $\frac{61}{9}$

   G. $\frac{52}{9}$

   H. $\frac{63}{9}$

   Difficulty: Hard

5. $10\frac{8}{9} =$ _____

   A. $\frac{89}{9}$

   B. $\frac{91}{9}$

   C. $\frac{98}{9}$

   D. $\frac{90}{9}$

   Difficulty: Hard

6. $\frac{7}{10} =$ _____

   E. 0.07

   F. 7

   G. 0.7

   H. 0.007

   Difficulty: Moderate

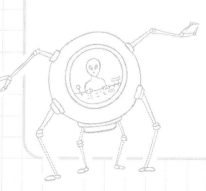

7. $\dfrac{64}{100}$ = _____

    A. 64   C. 0.064

    B. 0.64   D. 0.0064

Difficulty: Moderate

8. $\dfrac{4}{100}$ = _____

    E. 0.04   G. 0.004

    F. 0.4   H. 4

Difficulty: Moderate

9. 0.02 = _____

    A. $\dfrac{2}{10}$ C. $\dfrac{2}{100}$

    B. $\dfrac{1}{2}$ D. 2

Difficulty: Moderate

10. 0.8 = _____

    E. $\dfrac{1}{8}$ G. 8

    F. $\dfrac{8}{100}$ H. $\dfrac{8}{10}$

Difficulty: Moderate

1. Determine if **0.39** is 'more', 'less', or 'equal' to half.

   A. more than half
   B. less than half
   C. equal to half

   Difficulty: Easy

2. Determine if **0.69** is 'more', 'less', or 'equal' to half.

   D. more than half
   E. less than half
   F. equal to half

   Difficulty: Easy

3. Determine if **0.17** is 'more', 'less', or 'equal' to half.

   A. more than half
   B. less than half
   C. equal to half

   Difficulty: Easy

4. Determine if **0.88** is 'more', 'less', or 'equal' to half.

   D. more than half
   E. less than half
   F. equal to half

   Difficulty: Easy

5. Determine if **0.5** is 'more', 'less', or 'equal' to half.

   A. more than half
   B. less than half
   C. equal to half

   Difficulty: Easy

6. What is the value of the underlined digit, <u>5</u>4,949.5?

   E. 40,000   **G.** 50,000
   F. 60,000   **H.** 70,000

   Difficulty: Moderate

7. What is the value of the underlined digit, <u>7</u>33,068.245?

   A. 700   **C.** 70,000
   B. 7,000   **D.** 700,000

   Difficulty: Moderate

8. What is the value of the underlined digit, 6,630.<u>9</u>?

   E. 900   **G.** $\frac{9}{10}$

   F. 90   **H.** $\frac{9}{100}$

   Difficulty: Moderate

65

9. Katrina downloaded two apps which were 12.48 kb total. If one app was 1.98 kb, how big was the other app?

A. 1.5 C. 15
B. 10.5 D. 14.46

Difficulty: Moderate

10. Renee was buying food for her birthday party. She bought a 63.55 oz bag of barbeque chips and a 63.9 oz bag of salt and vinegar chips. How many ounces did she buy all together?

E. 127.5 G. 127.35
F. 127.45 H. 127.4

Difficulty: Moderate

11. Ramone walked 5.02 kilometers during the two days he was at the fair. On the first day he walked 1.52 kilometers. How far did he walk the second day?

A. 3.5 C. 1.52
B. 3.1 D. 2.5

Difficulty: Moderate

12. Antonio bought 7.91 lbs of grape and lemon jelly beans for his birthday party. If 4.81 lbs were grape flavor, how many pounds were lemon flavor?

E. 1.3 G. 3
F. 2.3 H. 3.1

Difficulty: Moderate

13. On Monday and Tuesday the lake received 8.73 inches of water. If it received 6.63 inches on Monday, how much did it receive on Tuesday?

A. 1.2 C. 2.2
B. 2.1 D. 1.6

Difficulty: Moderate

14. Sherese was measuring how much taller she got over two years. In the first year she grew 2.27 cm. In the second year she grew 7.8 cm. How much taller did she get altogether?

E. 10.70 G. 10.07
F. 10.7 H. 10

Difficulty: Moderate

1. A computer programmer had two files. The first was 34.89 gigabyes and the second was 38.9 gigabytes. What is the total file size of both?

    A. 77.39   **C.** 73.99

    B. 73.79   **D.** 79.37

Difficulty: Moderate

2. $4.57 \times 4.2 =$ _____

    E. 191.94   **G.** 1.9194

    F. 19.194   **H.** 1919.4

Difficulty: Difficult

3. $4.61 \times 1.1 =$ _____

    A. 50.71   **C.** 5.071

    B. 507.1   **D.** 5071

Difficulty: Hard

4. $7.335 \times 8.2 =$ _____

    E. 60.1470   **G.** 601.470

    F. 6.01470   **H.** 6014.70

Difficulty: Hard

5. $4.95 \times 4.2 =$ _____

    A. 2.0790   **C.** 20.790

    B. 207.90   **D.** 20790

Difficulty: Hard

6. $1.87 \times 8.3 =$ _____

    E. 1.5521   **G.** 1552.1

    F. 155.21   **H.** 15.521

Difficulty: Hard

7. $723.1 \div 10^2 =$ _____

    A. 72.31   **C.** 7.231

    B. 723.1   **D.** 7231

Difficulty: Moderate

8. $23.976 \times 10^4 =$ _____

    E. 2.39760   **G.** 23.9760

    F. 239,760   **H.** 23.976

Difficulty: Moderate

9. $83.7 \div 10^3 =$ _____

    A. 0.0837   **C.** 837

    B. 8.37   **D.** 8.37

Difficulty: Moderate

10. $56.461 \times 10^2 =$ _____

 E. 5.6461 G. 5,646.1

 F. 566.61 H. 56,461

 Difficulty: Moderate

11. $2.684 \div 10^1 =$ _____

 A. 2.684 C. 26.84

 B. 0.2684 D. 268.4

 Difficulty: Moderate

12. $814.1 \times$ _____ $= 814,100$

 E. 10 G. 1,000

 F. 100 H. 10,000

 Difficulty: Moderate

13. _____ $\times 1,000 = 408,627$

 A. 4.08627 C. 4086.27

 B. 40.8627 D. 408.627

 Difficulty: Moderate

14. $924.52 \times 100 =$ _____

 E. 9245.2 G. 924.52

 F. 92,452 H. 0.92452

 Difficulty: Moderate

15. $2,851.82 \div 10 =$ _____

 A. 28.5182 C. 2.85182

 B. 285.182 D. 0.285182

 Difficulty: Moderate

16. $32.9 \times$ _____ $= 32,900$

 E. 1,000 G. 10,000

 F. 10 H. 100

 Difficulty: Moderate

1. $6.5 \overline{)6804}$

   A. 1046 R 45

   C. 10.46 R 45

   D. 104.6 R 45

   B. 1047 R 4

Difficulty: Hard

2. $.65 \overline{)7365.995}$

   E. 113.323   **G.** 1.13323

   F. 1133.23   **H.** 11332.3

Difficulty: Hard

3. 49.56 + 45.3 = _____

   A. 94.86   **C.** 9486

   B. 9.486   **D.** 948.6

Difficulty: Moderate

4. 85.06 - 5.806 = _____

   E. 7.9254   **G.** 79.254

   F. 792.54   **H.** 79,254

Difficulty: Moderate

5. 71.5 + 76.8 = _____

   A. 1.483   **C.** 14.83

   B. 148.3   **D.** 1483

Difficulty: Moderate

6. 5,307 ÷ 0.87 = _____

   E. 6.100   **G.** 61.0

   F. 6,100   **H.** 0.6100

Difficulty: Hard

7. 117.8 ÷ 6.2 = _____

   A. 1.90   **C.** 0.0190

   B. 0.19   **D.** 19

Difficulty: Hard

8. Which option shows the numbers ordered from smallest to largest?

   E. 5.13, 5.76, 5.9, 5.91

   F. 5.39, 5.38, 5.36, 5

   G. 7.2, 7.4, 7.45, 7

   H. 7.63, 7.64, 7.6, 7.36

Difficulty: Moderate

9. Which option shows the numbers ordered from largest to smallest?

   A. 2.7, 2.9, 2.4, 2.41

   B. 1.73, 1.32, 1.3, 1.2

   C. 3.88, 3.5, 3.74, 3.98

   D. 3.68, 3.7, 3.25, 4

Difficulty: Moderate

10. Daniel filled a pitcher up **0.4** full then poured **0.08** of the pitcher into a glass. What amount of the total pitcher did he pour into the glass?

E. 0.032   G. 0.12

F. 1.2   H. 0.32

Difficulty: Moderate

11. An air freshener used **3.16** milliliters of perfume. If Janet wanted to make **4** air fresheners, how many milliliters of perfume would she use?

A. 1.264   C. 126.4

B. 1,264   D. 12.64

Difficulty: Moderate

12. Will was checking how much power his lights used. His first light by itself used **73.15** amps. When he turned on the second light, together they used **152.95** amps. How many amps did just the second light use?

E. 226.1   G. 79.8

F. 798   H. 7.98

Difficulty: Moderate

13. Sophia was checking the weight of a gold nugget and a piece of fools' gold. Together they weighed **98.06** grams. If the fools' gold was **20.16** grams, how much did the gold nugget weigh?

A. 7.79   C. 77.9

B. 118.22   D. 11.822

Difficulty: Moderate

1. A scientist was measuring the daily sodium values of different foods. If a soda has **44.22%** the daily value and fries have **49.1%** the daily value, how much would they have together?

   E. 4.88   G. 9.332

   F. 93.32   H. 488

   Difficulty: Moderate

2. A weatherman was measuring the amount of rain two cities received over a week. City A received **5.54** inches while City B received **4.2** inches. How much rain did they get total?

   A. 1.34   C. 0.974

   B. 13.4   D. 9.74

   Difficulty: Moderate

3. Which of the following number sentences is true?

   E. 5.76 < 5.67   G. 3.57 > 3.75

   F. 2.35 = 2.53   H. 5.73 > 5.37

   Difficulty: Hard

4. Which of the following number sentences is true?

   A. 3.65 < 3.56   C. 1.84 < 1.48

   B. 1.2 = 1.20   D. 3.79 > 3.97

   Difficulty: Hard

5. Which of the following number sentences is true?

   E. 5.69 = 5.96   G. 1.34 = 1.43

   F. 1.85 < 1.58   H. 3.14 < 3.41

   Difficulty: Hard

6. Which number has the least value?

   A. 6.51   C. 51.6

   B. 61.5   D. 5.16

   Difficulty: Moderate

7. Which number has the greatest value?

   E. 0.17   G. 70.1

   F. 07.1   H. 17.0

   Difficulty: Moderate

Measurement and Data

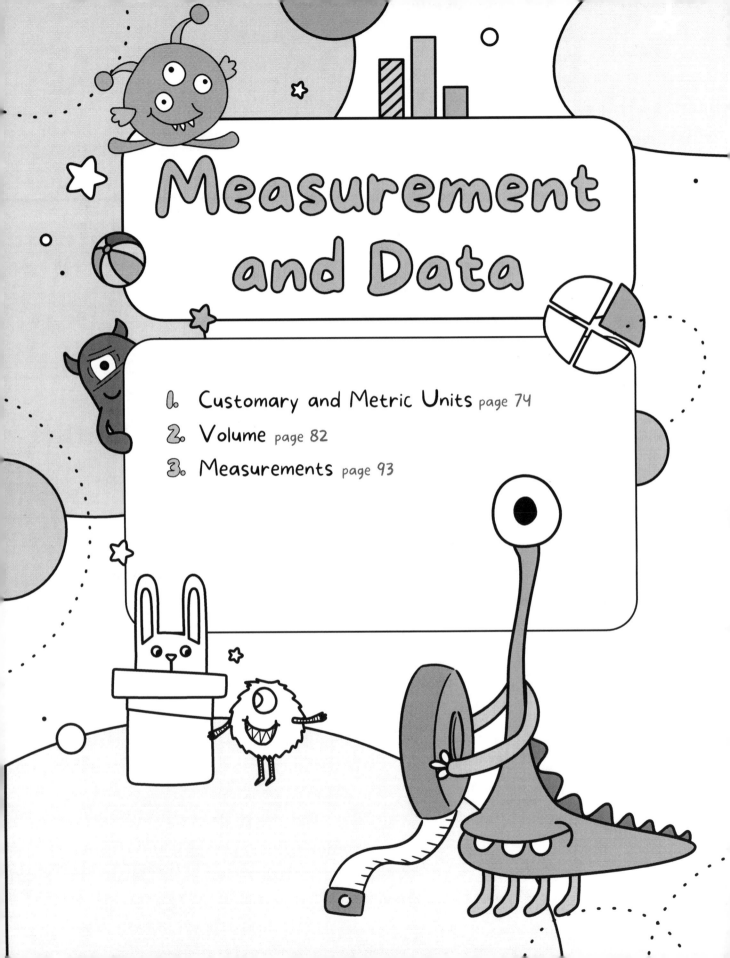

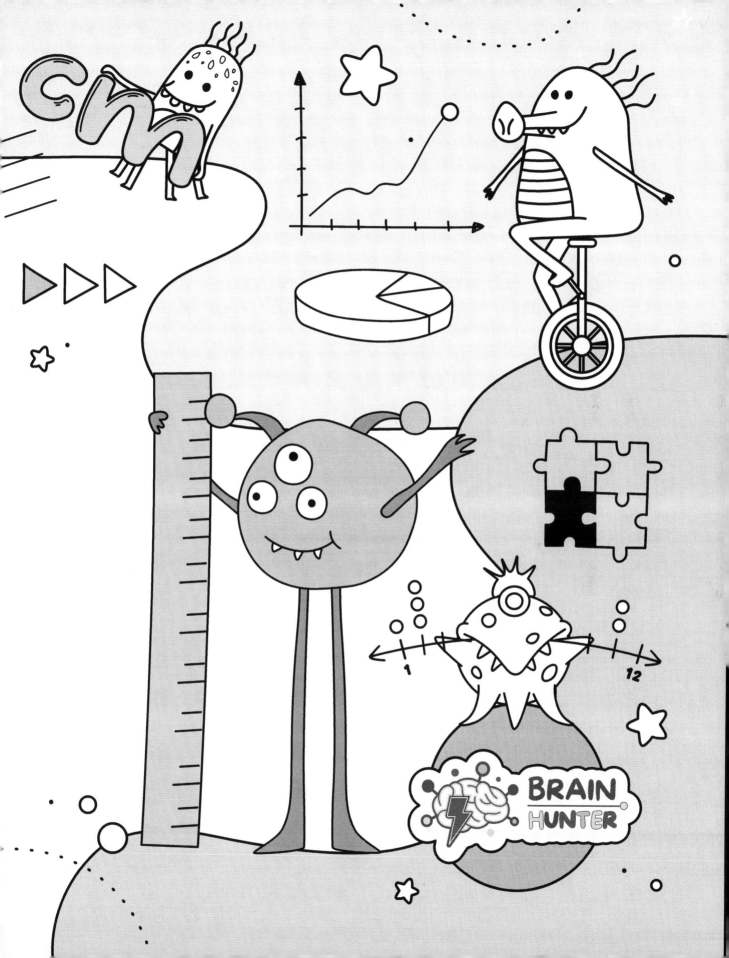

Conversion Chart

Customary Length	
12 in	1 ft
3 ft	1 yd
1760 yd	1 mi

Customary Weight	
16 oz	1 lb
2000 lb	1 ton

Customary Capacity	
8 fl oz	1 c
2 c	1 pt
2 pt	1 q
4 q	1 gal

Metric Length	
10 mm	1 cm
100 cm	1 m
1000 m	1 km

Metric Mass	
1000 mg	1 g
1000 g	1 kg

Metric Capacity	
1000 ml	1 L

1. Which is a better estimate for the length of a golf club?

A. 35 inches
B. 35 yards
C. 35 quarts
D. 35 gallons

Difficulty: Easy

2. Which is a better estimate for the height of a telephone pole?

E. 8 yards
G. 8 miles
F. 8 inches
H. 8 pounds

Difficulty: Easy

3. _____ yards = 108 inches

A. 2
C. 3
B. 4
D. 5

Difficulty: Moderate

4. Which is more, 1 ton or 230 pounds?

E. 1 ton
F. 230 pounds

Difficulty: Moderate

5. _____ pints = 1 gallon

A. 4
C. 8
B. 6
D. 2

Difficulty: Moderate

6. Which is more, 1 pint or 3 cups?

E. 1 pint
F. 3 cups

Difficulty: Moderate

7. Which is more, 1 tablespoon or 1 teaspoon?

A. 1 tablespoon
B. 1 teaspoon

Difficulty: Moderate

8. 14,319 lb = _____ T and _____ lb

E. 1 T and 319 lb
F. 2 T and 305 lb
G. 3 T 310 lb
H. 7 T 319 lb

Difficulty: Moderate

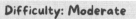

75

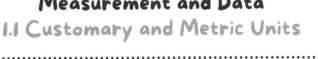

9. Which is a better estimate for the length of a peanut?

   A. 8 kilometers
   B. 8 millimeters
   C. 8 centimeters
   D. 8 hectometers

   Difficulty: Moderate

10. Which is a better estimate for the volume of a bathroom sink?

   E. 5 millimeters
   F. 5 liters
   G. 5 grams
   H. 5 kilograms

   Difficulty: Moderate

11. Del bought a cookie sheet for $8.07. He paid $8.55. How much change did Del receive?

   A. $0.48
   B. $0.55
   C. $0.38
   D. $0.42

   Difficulty: Moderate

12. Stephanie bought a roll of wrapping paper that cost $3.60. She gave the cashier $6.36. How much change did the cashier give back to Stephanie?

   E. $2.76
   F. $1.76
   G. $0.76
   H. $0.96

   Difficulty: Moderate

13. Heddy purchased a cherry pie for $5.24. She paid $5.86. How much change did Heddy receive?

   A. $0.62   **C.** $1.62
   B. $2.62   **D.** $1.42

   Difficulty: Moderate

14. The hotel is 22.7 miles west of the harbor, and the harbor is 54 miles west of the grocery store. How far apart are the grocery store and the hotel?

   E. 66.2 miles   **G.** 76.7 miles
   F. 75.2 miles   **H.** 68.4 miles

   Difficulty: Moderate

1. 5 feet = _____ inches

   E. 12   G. 60
   F. 40   H. 17

   Difficulty: Moderate

2. 4 feet = _____ inches

   A. 48   C. 84
   B. 36   D. 12

   Difficulty: Moderate

3. 6 feet = _____ yards

   E. 12   G. 3
   F. 4   H. 2

   Difficulty: Moderate

4. _____ feet = 4 yards

   A. 6   C. 12
   B. 8   D. 10

   Difficulty: Moderate

5. 4 feet and 11 inches = _____ inches

   E. 48   G. 32
   F. 59   H. 43

   Difficulty: Hard

6. 3 yards and 3 feet = _____ feet

   A. 9   C. 11
   B. 12   D. 8

   Difficulty: Hard

7. Which is more, 4 liters or 3,998 milliliters?

   E. 4 liters
   F. 3,998 milliliters
   G. they are equal

   Difficulty: Hard

8. Which is more, 10,000 milliliters or 10 liters?

   A. 10,000 milliliters
   B. 10 liters
   C. they are equal

   Difficulty: Hard

9. A pair of sunglasses weighs 2 ounces. Do 13 pairs of sunglasses weigh more than 1 pound?

   A. yes   B. no

   Difficulty: Hard

10. 8 fluid ounces = _____ pints

E. $\frac{1}{2}$ G. $\frac{1}{8}$

F. $\frac{1}{4}$ H. $\frac{1}{5}$

Difficulty: Hard

11. 2 fluid ounces = _____ cups

A. $\frac{1}{3}$ C. $\frac{1}{4}$

B. $\frac{1}{8}$ D. $\frac{1}{2}$

Difficulty: Hard

12. 1 gallon is about equal to 3.79 liters. 2 gallons is about equal to _____ liters.

E. 6.25   G. 7.50

F. 7.58   H. 6.55

Difficulty: Hard

13. What is the temperature of a bowl of ice cream?

A. 30°C   B. 30°F

Difficulty: Hard

14. Which is a better estimate for the length of a couch?

C. 10 yards   E. 10 feet
D. 10 miles   F. 10 inches

Difficulty: Moderate

15. A hot dog is 7 inches long. If you place 5 hot dogs in a line, will they be longer than 4 feet?

A. Yes   B. No

Difficulty: Moderate

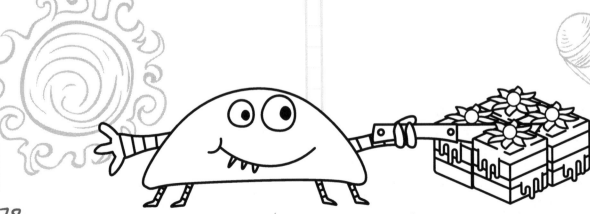

1. A bottle of nail polish has a volume of **3** teaspoons. Is the volume of **3** nail polish bottles greater than **4** tablespoons?

   A. Yes
   B. No

   Difficulty: Moderate

2. Which is more, 1 centimeter or 9 millimeters?

   A. 1 centimeter
   B. 9 millimeters
   C. They are equal

   Difficulty: Moderate

3. Which is more, 1 meter or 1,391 millimeters?

   A. 1 meter
   B. 1,391 millimeters
   C. They are equal

   Difficulty: Moderate

4. Add: 2 m 67 cm + 6 m 13 cm = _____ m _____ cm

   A. 8m 80 cm
   B. 8m 60cm
   C. 8m 45cm
   D. 8m 70cm

   Difficulty: Hard

5. Add: 2 cm 3 mm + 1 cm 4 mm = _____ cm _____ mm

   A. 5cm 2 mm
   B. 4cm 6mm
   C. 3cm 5mm
   D. 3cm 7mm

   Difficulty: Hard

6. Which is about equal to 1 teaspoon?

   A. 5 liters
   B. 5 gallons
   C. 5 cups
   D. 5 milliliters

   Difficulty: Moderate

7. A cereal box holds a volume of 5 quarts. Is the volume of 3 cereal boxes greater than 3 gallons?

    A. yes

    B. no

                  Difficulty: Hard

8. 24 in = _____ ft _____ in

    A. 2 ft 2 in

    B. 2 ft 12 in

    C. 2 ft 8 in

    D. 2 ft

                  Difficulty: Moderate

9. 3 lb 8 oz = _____ oz

    A. 56   **C.** 48

    B. 65   **D.** 64

                  Difficulty: Moderate

10. 13 c = _____ pt _____ c

    A. 6 pt 2 c

    B. 6 pt 1 c

    C. 5 pt 1 c

    D. 6 pt

                  Difficulty: Moderate

11. A toad weighs 6 ounces. Do 8 toads weigh more than 2 pounds?

    A. Yes   **B.** No

                  Difficulty: Moderate

12. 3 quarts = _____ pints

    A. 4

    B. 5

    C. 6

    D. 8

                  Difficulty: Moderate

13. _____ quarts = 14 pints

    A. 12

    B. 9

    C. 8

    D. 7

                  Difficulty: Moderate

14. 12 quarts = _____ gallons

    A. 24

    B. 4

    C. 3

    D. 48

                  Difficulty: Moderate

1. Hermann goes to a pumpkin patch and picks out a pumpkin that has a mass of **6,000** grams. How many kilograms is the pumpkin?

E. 6 kg   G. 10 kg

F. 4 kg   H. 8 kg

Difficulty: Moderate

2. If one paperclip has the mass of 1 gram and 1,000 paperclips have a mass of 1 kilogram, how many kilograms are 8,000 paperclips?

A. 6   C. 8

B. 10   D. 1,000

Difficulty: Moderate

3. Spencer's eraser has a mass of **20** grams. How many milligrams are in 20 grams?

E. 20,000   G. 200

F. 2,000   H. 20

Difficulty: Moderate

4. Etienne goes to the grocery store and is looking at a winter squash. It has a mass of 1.8 kilograms. How many grams is the winter squash?

A. 180   C. 18

B. 1,800   D. 18,000

Difficulty: Moderate

5. A box contains 4 bags of sugar. The total mass of all 4 bags is 6 kg. What is the mass of each bag in grams?

E. 24 grams
F. 1,500 grams
G. 1,200 grams
H. 2,500 grams

Difficulty: Moderate

6. 6 feet = _____ yards

A. 12   C. 6

B. 3   D. 2

Difficulty: Moderate

7. _____ inches = 8 feet

E. 60   G. 96

F. 80   H. 106

Difficulty: Moderate

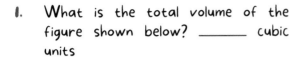

1. What is the total volume of the figure shown below? _____ cubic units

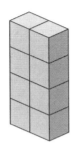

A. 6   C. 2

B. 8   D. 4

Difficulty: Easy

2. What is the total volume of the figure shown below? _____ cubic units

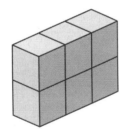

E. 2   G. 6

F. 3   H. 4

Difficulty: Easy

3. What is the total volume of the figure shown below? _____ cubic units

A. 5   C. 20

B. 2   D. 10

Difficulty: Easy

4. What is the total volume of the figure shown below? _____ cubic units

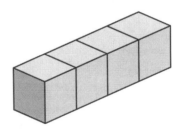

E. 4   G. 8

F. 1   H. 2

Difficulty: Easy

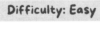

5. What is the total volume of the figure shown below? _____ cubic units

A. 10   C. 12

B. 5   D. 1

Difficulty: Easy

6. What is the total volume of the figure shown below? _____ cubic units

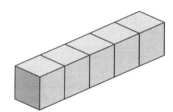

E. 5   G. 10

F. 1   H. 2

Difficulty: Easy

7. What is the total volume of the figure shown below? _____ cubic units

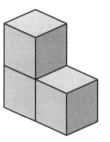

A. 6   C. 4

B. 2   D. 3

Difficulty: Moderate

8. What is the total volume of the figure shown below? _____ cubic units

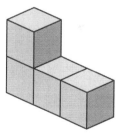

E. 2   G. 4

F. 8   H. 6

Difficulty: Moderate

1. What is the total volume of the figure shown below? _____ cubic units

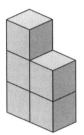

   A. 5   C. 2
   B. 4   D. 10

   Difficulty: Moderate

2. What is the total volume of the figure shown below? _____ cubic units

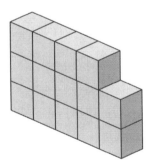

   E. 12   G. 10
   F. 14   H. 16

   Difficulty: Moderate

3. What is the total volume of the figure shown below? _____ cubic units

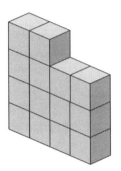

   A. 12   C. 14
   B. 15   D. 28

   Difficulty: Moderate

4. What is the width of the figure shown below?

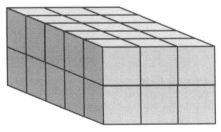

   E. 3   G. 4
   F. 5   H. 2

   Difficulty: Moderate

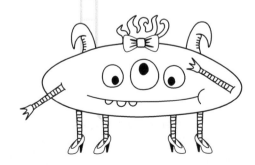

5. What is the length of the figure shown below?

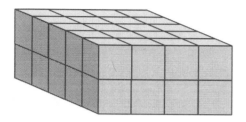

A. 5   **C.** 2
B. 4   **D.** 40

Difficulty: Moderate

6. What is the height of the figure shown below?

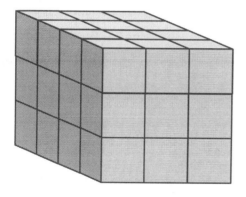

E. 4   **G.** 2
F. 3   **H.** 36

Difficulty: Moderate

7. What is the length of the figure shown below?

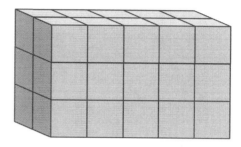

A. 2   **C.** 3
B. 5   **D.** 30

Difficulty: Moderate

8. What is the height of the figure shown below?

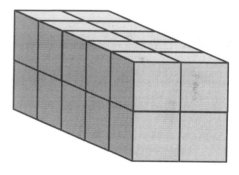

E. 5   **G.** 4
F. 2   **H.** 20

Difficulty: Moderate

9. What is the volume of the figure shown below? _____ cubic units

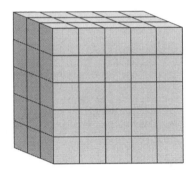

A. 55   C. 50

B. 65   D. 75

Difficulty: Hard

10. What is the width of the figure shown below?

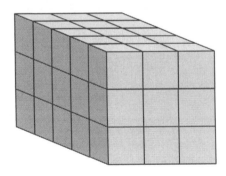

E. 5   G. 8

F. 3   H. 6

Difficulty: Moderate

11. What is the length of the figure shown below?

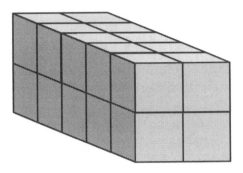

A. 5   C. 4

B. 2   D. 20

Difficulty: Moderate

12. What is the height of the figure shown below?

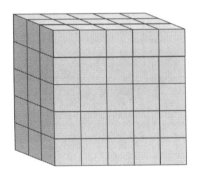

E. 3   G. 5

F. 9   H. 25

Difficulty: Moderate

1. What is the volume of a figure with that is 4 inches wide, 8 inches tall, and 10 inches long?

   A. 22 in³   C. 220 in³

   B. 320 in³   D. 120 in³

   Difficulty: Hard

2. A rectangular prism has a width of 4 cm, a height of 5 cm, and a length of 6 cm. What is the volume of the prism?

   E. 240 cm³   G. 60 cm³

   F. 110 cm³   H. 120 cm³

   Difficulty: Hard

3. A rectangular prism has a width of 9 cm, a height of 7 cm, and a depth of 4 cm. What is the volume of the prism?

   A. 125 cm³   C. 252 cm³

   B. 232 cm³   D. 240 cm³

   Difficulty: Hard

4. What is the volume of a figure with that is 6 inches wide, 7 inches tall, and 6 inches long?

   E. 252 in³   G. 262 in³

   F. 126 in³   H. 116 in³

   Difficulty: Hard

5. A rectangular prism has a width of 9 cm, a height of 4 cm, and a length of 6 cm. What is the volume of the prism?

   A. 116 cm³   C. 216 cm³

   B. 432 cm³   D. 126 cm³

   Difficulty: Hard

6. What is the volume of a figure with that is 10 inches wide, 5 inches tall, and 10 inches long?

   E. 500 in³   G. 125 in³

   F. 250 in³   H. 50,000 in³

   Difficulty: Hard

7. A rectangular prism has a width of 9 cm, a height of 5 cm, and a length of 7 cm. What is the volume of the prism?

   A. 325 cm³   C. 305 cm³

   B. 315 cm³   D. 225 cm³

   Difficulty: Hard

8. A rectangular prism has a width of 8 cm, a height of 5 cm, and a length of 2 cm. What is the volume of the prism?

   E. 40 cm³   G. 60 cm³

   F. 120 cm³   H. 80 cm³

   Difficulty: Hard

9. What is the volume of a figure with that is 9 inches wide, 3 inches tall, and 3 inches long?

   A. 86 in³   C. 81 in³
   B. 121 in³   D. 71 in³

   Difficulty: Hard

10. What is the volume of a figure with that is 3 inches wide, 2 inches tall, and 5 inches long?

   E. 15 in³   G. 40 in³
   F. 60 in³   H. 30 in³

   Difficulty: Hard

11. Which of the following expressions could be used to determine the volume of the box?

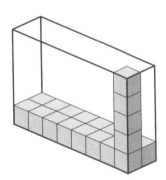

   A. 8 × 2 × 5   C. 5 × 2 × 5
   B. 6 × 2 × 5   D. 9 × 2 × 5

   Difficulty: Hard

12. Which of the following expressions could be used to determine the volume of the box?

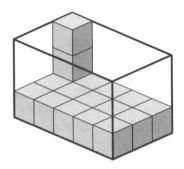

   E. 3 × 4 × 3   G. 5 × 2 × 3
   F. 5 × 3 × 3   H. 9 × 3 × 3

   Difficulty: Hard

13. Which of the following expressions could be used to determine the volume of the box?

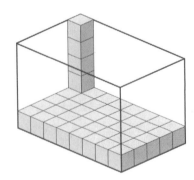

   A. 9 × 5 × 5   C. 8 × 5 × 4
   B. 7 × 8 × 5   D. 8 × 5 × 5

   Difficulty: Hard

1. Which of the following expressions could be used to determine the volume of the box?

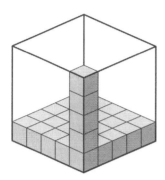

E. 5 × 5 × 5   G. 5 × 5 × 6

F. 4 × 5 × 4   H. 5 × 4 × 6

Difficulty: Hard

2. Which of the following expressions could be used to determine the volume of the box?

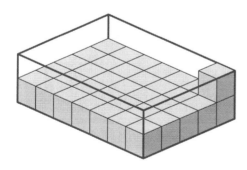

A. 6 × 4 × 2   C. 7 × 5 × 2

B. 7 × 3 × 2   D. 8 × 4 × 2

Difficulty: Hard

3. Lindsay has a box to keep her beads in and the length is 12 cm, height 8 cm, and width 6 cm. Find the volume of the box.

E. 216 cm³   G. 96 cm³

F. 576 cm³   H. 48 cm³

Difficulty: Hard

4. Jim made a rectangular prism whose length is 4 in., height 10 in., and width 6 in. Find the volume of the rectangular prism.

A. 24 in³   C. 60 in³

B. 64 in³   D. 240 in³

Difficulty: Hard

5. An aquarium is 90 m long and 60 m wide. What is the volume of the water in the tank, if the depth of water is 30 m?

E. 57,000 m³
F. 162,000 m³
G. 324,000 m³
H. 90,000 m³

Difficulty: Hard

6. A swimming pool in a community is **20** yd wide, **30** yd long, and **4** yd deep. What is the volume of the pool?

   A. 2,400 yd³
   B. 800 yd³
   C. 120 yd³
   D. 24,000 yd³

   Difficulty: Hard

7. A rectangular prism is **4** m long, **3** m wide, and **80** m high. Find the volume of the rectangular prism.

   E. 0.96 m³   **G.** 960 cm²
   F. 960 m³   **H.** 9.6 m³

   Difficulty: Hard

8. A rectangular swimming pool is built with the dimensions **13** m × **6** m × **4** m. Calculate the volume of the pool.

   A. 288 m³   **C.** 312 m³
   B. 308 m³   **D.** 46 m³

   Difficulty: Hard

9. What is the height of the figure below? _____ unit cubes

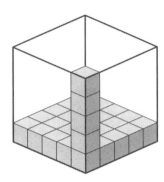

   E. 6   **G.** 4
   F. 5   **H.** 7

   Difficulty: Moderate

10. What is the width of the figure below? _____ unit cubes

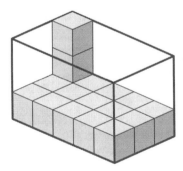

   A. 3   **C.** 4
   B. 2   **D.** 15

   Difficulty: Moderate

1. What is the length of the figure below? _____ unit cubes

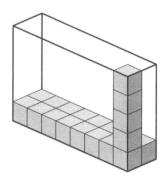

E. 5   G. 7

F. 6   H. 8

Difficulty: Moderate

3. What is the length of the figure below? _____ unit cubes

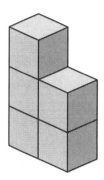

E. 2   G. 5

F. 3   H. 6

Difficulty: Moderate

2. What is the height of the figure below? _____ unit cubes

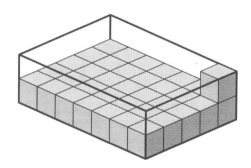

A. 3   C. 7

B. 6   D. 2

Difficulty: Moderate

4. What is the volume of a figure with that is 5 inches wide, 5 inches tall, and 4 inches long?

A. 120 in³   C. 100 in³

B. 110 in³   D. 150 in³

Difficulty: Moderate

5. What is the volume of a figure with that is 5 inches wide, 10 inches tall, and 3 inches long?

E. 90 in³   G. 125 in³

F. 110 in³   H. 150 in³

Difficulty: Moderate

6. A rectangular prism has a width of 3 cm, a height of 4 cm, and a depth of 10 cm. What is the volume of the prism?

    A. 110 cm³   **C.** 120 cm³

    B. 100 cm³   **D.** 80 cm³

      Difficulty: Moderate

7. Which of the following expressions could be used to determine the volume of the box?

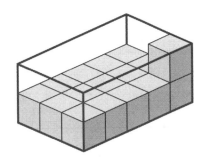

    E. 2 x 4 x 6   **G.** 3 x 5 x 2

    F. 3 x 5 x 1   **H.** 2 x 3 x 4

      Difficulty: Hard

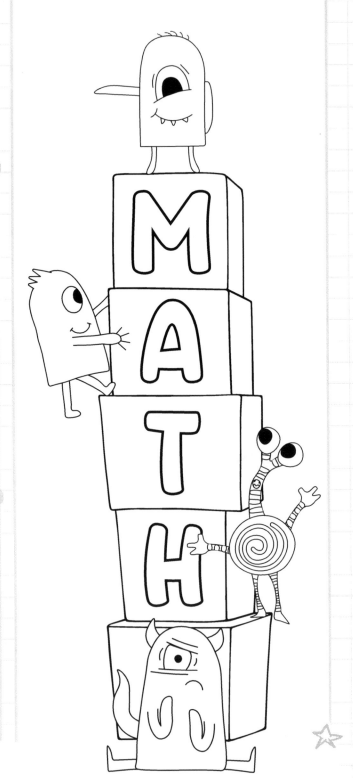

1. What is the perimeter of the rectangle? _____ inches

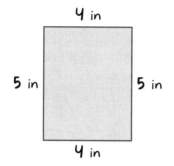

4 in

5 in   5 in

4 in

E. 25   G. 18

F. 20   H. 22

Difficulty: Moderate

2. What is the perimeter of the rectangle? _____ yds

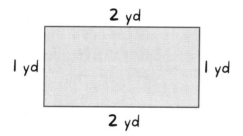

2 yd

1 yd   1 yd

2 yd

A. 5   C. 4

B. 8   D. 6

Difficulty: Moderate

3. What is the perimeter of the rectangle? _____ cm

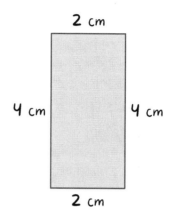

2 cm

4 cm   4 cm

2 cm

E. 6   G. 8

F. 12   H. 10

Difficulty: Moderate

4. The perimeter of a rectangular ink pad is **30** centimeters. The area is **50** square centimeters. What are the dimensions of the ink pad?

A. 3 centimeters by 7 centimeters

B. 5 centimeters by 5 centimeters

C. 5 centimeters by 10 centimeters

D. 3 centimeters by 5 centimeters

Difficulty: Hard

5. The area of a worksheet is 48 square inches. The perimeter is 28 inches. What are the dimensions of the worksheet?

   E. 2 in by 24 in
   F. 4 in by 12 in
   G. 6 in by 8 in
   H. 4 in by 8 in

   Difficulty: Hard

6. What is the measurement of this angle?

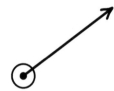

   A. 270°   C. 90°
   B. 360°   D. 180°

   Difficulty: Hard

7. What is the measurement of this angle?

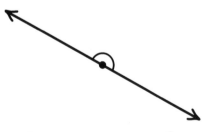

   E. $\frac{1}{4}$ turn   G. $\frac{3}{4}$ turn

   F. $\frac{1}{2}$ turn   H. 1 full turn

   Difficulty: Hard

8. What fraction of a turn is this angle?

   A. $\frac{1}{4}$ turn   C. $\frac{3}{4}$ turn

   B. $\frac{1}{2}$ turn   D. 1 full turn

   Difficulty: Hard

9. What is the measurement of this angle?

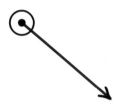

   E. 270°   G. 90°
   F. 360°   H. 180°

   Difficulty: Hard

10. What is the measure of this angle? Choose the best estimate.

A. 20°   **C.** 90°

B. 360°   **D.** 180°

Difficulty: Hard

11. What is the value of w?

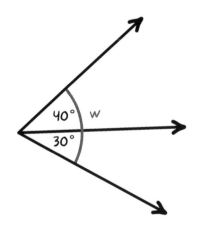

E. 90°   **G.** 70°

F. 10°   **H.** 120°

Difficulty: Moderate

12. What is the value of k?

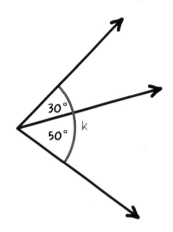

A. 90°   **C.** 60°

B. 80°   **D.** 70°

Difficulty: Moderate

13. What is the value of y?

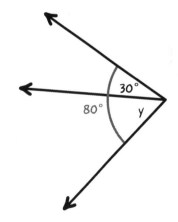

E. 40°   **G.** 30°

F. 50°   **H.** 60°

Difficulty: Moderate

14. What is the value of k?

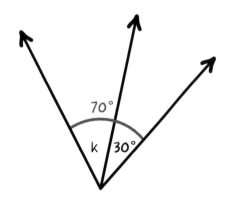

A. 40°   C. 30°

B. 50°   D. 60°

Difficulty: Moderate

15. What is the value of r?

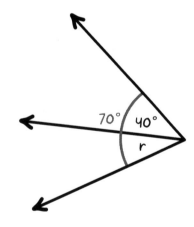

E. 40°   G. 30°

F. 50°   H. 20°

Difficulty: Moderate

16. What is the value of d?

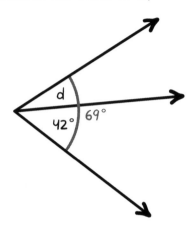

A. 42°   C. 30°

B. 27°   D. 22°

Difficulty: Hard

17. What is the value of f?

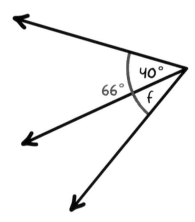

E. 42°   G. 10°

F. 26°   H. 22°

Difficulty: Hard

1. What is the value of c?

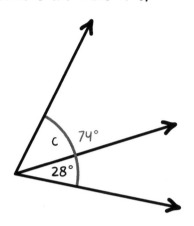

c 74°
28°

A. 32°   C. 46°
B. 26°   D. 42°

Difficulty: Hard

2. What is the value of j?

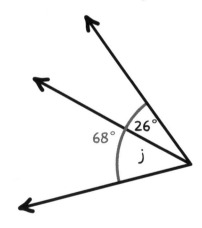

68° 26°
j

E. 42°   G. 46°
F. 26°   H. 22°

Difficulty: Hard

3. What is the value of m?

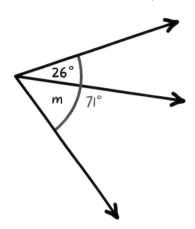

26°
m 71°

A. 32°   C. 46°
B. 45°   D. 42°

Difficulty: Hard

4. A water sprinkler covers **90°** of the lawn at the library. How many times will the sprinkler need to be moved to in order to cover the entire **360°** of the lawn?

E. 6   G. 4
F. 10   H. 8

Difficulty: Hard

5. A ceiling fan rotates **85°** and then stops. How many more degrees does it need to rotate in order to make a full rotation?

   A. 275   **C.** 125

   B. 150   **D.** 250

Difficulty: Hard

6. At ice skating lessons Amber attempts to do a **360°** spin but only manages a quarter turn. How many degrees short was Amber on her attempt?

   E. 250   **G.** 270

   F. 180   **H.** 190

Difficulty: Hard

7. A Ferris wheel makes **3** full rotations and then stops to let more riders on. How many total degrees did the Ferris wheel rotate before stopping?

   A. 1020   **C.** 360

   B. 270   **D.** 1080

Difficulty: Hard

8. What is the measure of this angle? Choose the best estimate.

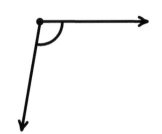

   E. 20°   **G.** 100°

   F. 60°   **H.** 180°

Difficulty: Hard

9. What is the measure of this angle? Choose the best estimate.

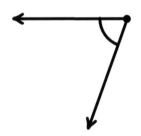

   A. 95°   **C.** 70°

   B. 145°   **D.** 20°

Difficulty: Hard

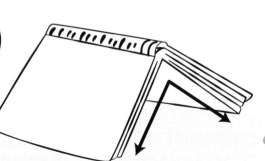

10. What is the measure of this angle? Choose the best estimate.

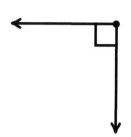

E. 90°   G. 120°

F. 60°   H. 180°

Difficulty: Hard

11. What is the measure of this angle? Choose the best estimate.

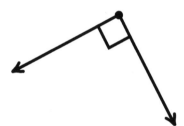

A. 90°   C. 120°

B. 60°   D. 180°

Difficulty: Hard

12. What is the measure of this angle? Choose the best estimate.

E. 120°   G. 0°

F. 180°   H. 360°

Difficulty: Hard

13. Is this angle acute, right, or obtuse?

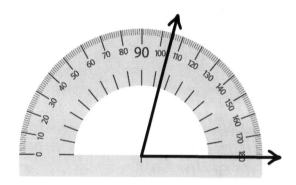

A. acute
B. right
C. obtuse

Difficulty: Hard

14. Is this angle acute, right, or obtuse?

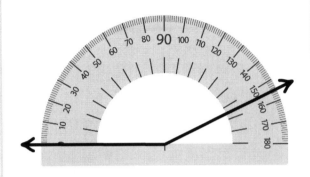

E. acute
F. right
G. obtuse

Difficulty: Hard

15. A restaurant added a new outdoor section that was 4 feet wide and 6 feet long. What is the area of their new outdoor section?

A. 18 ft² C. 10 ft²
B. 24 ft² D. 12 ft²

Difficulty: Moderate

16. An island in the Indian Ocean was 5 miles wide. It had a total area of 50 square miles. How long is the island?

E. 55 mi G. 45 mi
F. 250 mi H. 10 mi

Difficulty: Hard

1. Ansley was cutting out some fabric for a friend. She cut a piece that was **6** centimeters wide and **5** centimeters long. What is the area of the fabric she cut out?

A. 11 cm² **C.** 30 cm²

B. 1 cm² **D.** 36 cm²

Difficulty: Moderate

2. A rectangle had a length of **2** inches and a width of **4** inches. What is the area of the rectangle?

E. 6 in² **G.** 2 in²

F. 8 in² **H.** 10 in²

Difficulty: Moderate

3. A rug had a length of **7** feet and a total area of **35** ft². What is the width of the rug?

A. 7 ft **C.** 42 ft

B. 5 ft **D.** 4 ft

Difficulty: Hard

4. Daniel bought a cookie at a bake sale. If the cookie cost **$3.10** and he paid with a twenty dollar bill, how much change should he get back?

E. $16.90 **G.** $14.90

F. $12.90 **H.** $6.90

Difficulty: Moderate

5. Alexander bought a screw driver at a hardware store. If the screw driver cost **$3.60** and he paid with a ten dollar bill, how much change should he get back?

A. $16.40 **C.** $6.40

B. $12.40 **D.** $8.40

Difficulty: Moderate

6. Christian bought **3** popcorns, **1** soda, and **1** box of candy at the theater. The popcorns cost **$2.85** each, the soda cost **$4.50**, and the box of candy was **$2.50**. If he paid with **2** ten dollar bills, how much change should she get back?

E. $4.45   G. $4.50

F. $5.55   H. $5.45

Difficulty: Hard

7. Ashley bought **2** posters, **3** books, and **1** bookmark at the school book fair. The posters cost **$0.20** each, the books cost **$3.35**, a piece and the bookmark was **$3.55**. If she paid with a twenty dollar bill, how much change should she get back?

A. $4.00   C. $7.00

B. $5.00   D. $6.00

Difficulty: Hard

8. Madison's mom spent seven hundred eighty-one dollars and forty-five cents on new school supplies for her and her sisters. How would you write the amount she spent in numeric form?

E. $780.45   G. $791.45

F. $781.55   H. $781.45

Difficulty: Moderate

9. Heidi read online that a cell phone bill was four thousand, seven hundred eighty eight dollars and twenty-four cents. How would you write the bill amount as a number?

A. $4,788.24
C. $4,788.42

B. $4,878.24
D. $4,787.24

Difficulty: Moderate

10. What is the value of y?

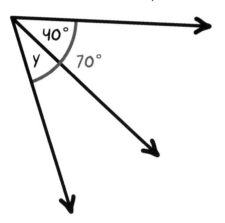

E. 40°
G. 20°

F. 30°
H. 110°

Difficulty: Moderate

11. What is the value of r?

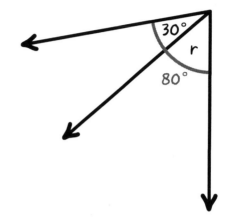

A. 50°
C. 110°

B. 20°
D. 100°

Difficulty: Moderate

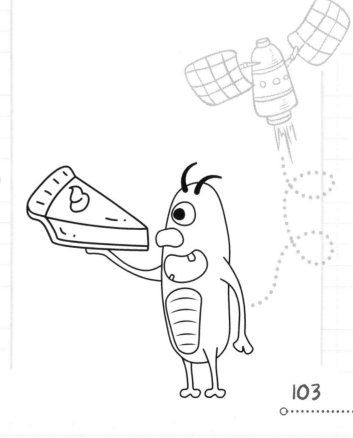

12. What is the value of g?

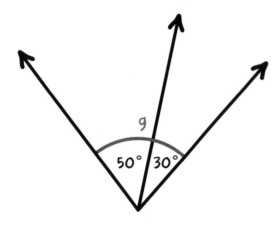

E. 20°	G. 80°
F. 100°	H. 60°

Difficulty: Moderate

14. What is the value of c?

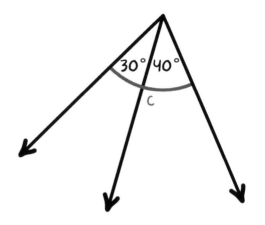

E. 120°	G. 50°
F. 70°	H. 80°

Difficulty: Moderate

13. What is the value of d?

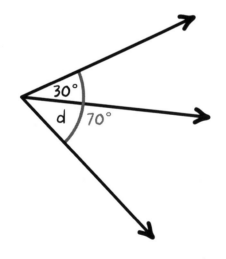

A. 20°	C. 100°
B. 50°	D. 40°

Difficulty: Moderate

15. What is the value of j?

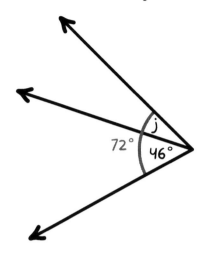

72° 46° j

A. 36°   C. 16°

B. 26°   D. 118°

Difficulty: Hard

16. Zack made oatmeal cookies to take to a party. It took him **55** minutes to make the dough and **45** minutes to bake all of the cookies. It was **2:50** P.M. when Zack finally took the last batch of cookies out of the oven. What time was it when Zack started making the cookies?

E. 2:05 pm   G. 2:35 pm

F. 2:20 pm   H. 1:10 pm

Difficulty: Hard

17. Daryl and his brother went to a soccer game on Saturday. They left the house at **6:10** P.M. It took **35** minutes to drive to the soccer field, and they arrived 1 hour before the game started. What time did the soccer game start?

A. 6:45 pm   C. 7:45 pm

B. 7:30 pm   D. 7:50 pm

Difficulty: Hard

Algebra

$\pi \approx 3.14$

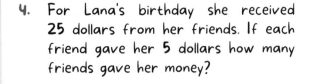

1. A pet store had **6** Siamese cats. If they sold **2** of them, how many cats do they still have?

   A. 8   C. 4
   B. 12   D. 2

   Difficulty: Easy

2. Each room in a new house needs to have **2** outlets. If the contractor buys **14** outlets, how many rooms are in the house?

   E. 28   G. 12
   F. 7   H. 16

   Difficulty: Easy

3. There are **7** different books in the 'All About Penguins' series. If you read **5** of the books, how many more do you still have to read?

   A. 2   C. 35
   B. 12   D. 9

   Difficulty: Easy

4. For Lana's birthday she received **25** dollars from her friends. If each friend gave her **5** dollars how many friends gave her money?

   E. 30   G. 5
   F. 20   H. 125

   Difficulty: Easy

5. Banks was helping his mom wash clothes. They washed **8** loads with **6** towels in each load. How many towels did they wash total?

   A. 14   C. 2
   B. 48   D. 24

   Difficulty: Easy

6. An architect was building a hotel downtown. He built it with **6** rooms in total. If there are **2** rooms on each story how many stories tall is the hotel?

   E. 8   G. 3
   F. 4   H. 6

   Difficulty: Easy

7. Maggie had **9** apps on her phone. To free up some space she deleted **6** of the apps. How many apps did she have left?

A. 9   **C.** 12

B. 15   **D.** 3

Difficulty: Easy

8. Robin collected **12** cans for recycling. If she put **9** cans in one bag how many cans did she have left?

E. 3   **G.** 21

F. 5   **H.** 12

Difficulty: Easy

9. A group of **6** friends were dressing as pirates for Halloween. If each costume cost **6** dollars, how much did they spend?

A. $12   **C.** $36

B. $18   **D.** $6

Difficulty: Easy

10. Ryan is helping to put away books. If he has **42** books to put away and each shelf can hold **7** books how many shelves will he need?

E. 49   **G.** 8

F. 7   **H.** 6

Difficulty: Easy

11. At the flea market Ringo found **2** buckets of LEGOs with each bucket containing **5,130** LEGO pieces. If he wanted to split the LEGO pieces into **6** piles, how many pieces should he put into each pile?

A. 1,710   **C.** 10,260

B. 3,420   **D.** 2,710

Difficulty: Moderate

12. At Odessa's bakery over the course of a year she sold **48** birthday cakes for $71 a cake. At the end of the year she determined that for each cake she sold she had spent 1/3 of the sale price on ingredients. How much money did she spend on ingredients for cakes?

E. $2,272   **G.** $1,136

F. $22   **H.** $142

Difficulty: Moderate

1. Reagan's mother had **28** small photo albums filled with **74** photos in each. In order to save some space she bought **2** larger albums with each album having **99** pages. If she wanted to put all her pictures into the large albums, with the same number of pictures in each, how many pictures should be in each album?

A. 1,036   C. 518
B. 2,072   D. 1,038

Difficulty: Moderate

2. Holly was planning to marathon watch episodes of her favorite show. The show had **48** episodes with each episode lasting exactly **22** minutes. If she planned to spend **4** days watching the show how many minutes should she watch each day?

E. 262   G. 26
F. 246   H. 264

Difficulty: Moderate

3. An industrial machine made **8,484** cans of diet sodas and **7** times as many regular sodas over the course of **47** minutes. The regular sodas were then placed into **4** shipping boxes with each shipping box containing the same number of sodas. How many regular sodas were in each shipping box?

A. 8,542   C. 14,847
B. 188   D. 235

Difficulty: Moderate

4. A restaurant owner bought **4** boxes of disposable cups for **$109**, with each box containing **2,632** cups. If he wanted to divvy up the cups among his **2** restaurants, with each restaurant getting the same number of cups, how many cups should each store get?

E. 5,264   G. 2,743
F. 2,741   H. 5,373

Difficulty: Moderate

5. Olivia was trying to save up $393. At her job she made $14 an hour and she worked 29 hours a week. After paying for her food and other expenditures she ended up only saving 1/2 of her weeks earnings. How much money did she save up each week?

A. 407

C. 203

B. 406

D. 43

Difficulty: Moderate

6. A contractor bought 59 boxes of nails at a price of $3 per box. Each box contained 21 nails. If he distributed the nails to the 3 houses he was building and made sure each house received the same number of nails, how many nails would each house get?

E. 413

G. 63

F. 411

H. 177

Difficulty: Moderate

7. Michael bought a new pair of skis for $350. He put $110 down and received a student discount of $30. His mother gave him 1/2 of the balance for his birthday. Which of these expressions could be used to find the amount Maxwell still owes on the skis?

A. $350-110+30 \div 2$

B. $350-(110-30) \div 2$

C. $[350-(110-30) \div 2]$

D. $[350-(110+30)] \div 2$

Difficulty: Hard

8. Rasheed had 12 rapalas. He gave some to Halima. Now he has 6 rapalas left. How many rapalas did Rasheed give to Halima?

E. 4

G. 18

F. 6

H. 22

Difficulty: Easy

9. Jessie had some apples. Adam gave her 6 more apples. Now she has 15 apples. How many apples did Jessie have to start with?

A. 6

C. 9

B. 21

D. 11

Difficulty: Moderate

1. Clayton has 12 tractors. He has 5 more tractors than Stan. How many tractors does Stan have?

   E. 7 G. 6

   F. 17 H. 60

   Difficulty: Moderate

2. Lukas has $8. Bertie has $9 more than Lukas. How much money does Bertie have?

   A. $2 C. $18

   B. $72 D. $17

   Difficulty: Moderate

3. Linnaea had some tangerines. She gave 7 to Maleah. Now she has 9 tangerines left. How many tangerines did Linnaea have to start with?

   E. 14 G. 2

   F. 16 H. 18

   Difficulty: Moderate

4. There are 49 pencils in the drawer. Kaz took 42 pencils from the drawer. How many pencils are now in the drawer?

   A. 91 C. 7

   B. 21 D. 9

   Difficulty: Moderate

5. There are 9 oak trees currently in the park. Park workers had to cut down 2 oak trees that were damaged. How many oak trees will be in the park when the workers are finished?

   E. 7 G. 18

   F. 9 H. 3

   Difficulty: Easy

6. Horatio bought 43 dozen eggs from the grocery store to bake some cakes. He plans to bake the cakes over 2 days. How many eggs did Keith buy?

   A. 89 C. 516

   B. 24 D. 45

   Difficulty: Hard

7. Lauryn has **3** books and she has read **8** total books. Meagan has **5** times more books than Lauryn. How many books does Meagan have?

E. 24   G. 40

F. 15   H. 16

Difficulty: Hard

8. Olivia had Pokemon cards and **4** had spots. She gave **9** away. She now has **2** Pokemon cards left. How many Pokemon cards did she start with?

A. 7   C. 6

B. 15   D. 11

Difficulty: Hard

9. Elaine has **36** muffins, which he needs to box up, **4** of which are strawberry, into dozens. How many boxes does she need?

E. 144   G. 40

F. 3   H. 10

Difficulty: Hard

10. Klintr has saved **1800** pennies from selling lemonade. How many dollars does Klintr have?

A. $18.00   C. $1,800.00

B. $180.00   D. $1.80

Difficulty: Hard

11. Christian bought **420** crayons that came in packs of **15**. There were **7** colors of crayons. How many packs of crayons did Fred buy?

E. 105   G. 28

F. 4   H. 22

Difficulty: Hard

12. Alisa had **46** nickels in her bank. She spent **12** of her nickels. How many nickels does she have now?

A. 58   C. 46

B. 552   D. 34

Difficulty: Easy

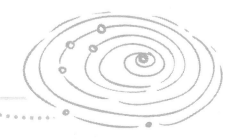

1. Maurice had **3** nickels in his bank. His dad gave him **7** nickels and **6** pennies. How many nickels does Maurice have now?

   E. 10   G. 9

   F. 16   H. 13

   Difficulty: Hard

2. Jana sold half of her comic books and then bought **7** more. She now has **14**. How many did she begin with?

   A. 14   C. 21

   B. 7   D. 28

   Difficulty: Hard

3. Drew bought **4** new baseball trading cards to add to his collection. The next day his dog ate half of his collection. There are now only **39** cards left. How many cards did Drew start with?

   E. 74   G. 86

   F. 43   H. 39

   Difficulty: Hard

4. Katrina bought a soft drink for **4** dollars and **7** candy bars. She spent a total of **32** dollars. How much did each candy bar cost?

   A. $4   C. $14

   B. $7   D. $32

   Difficulty: Hard

5. Kostya spent half of his allowance going to the movies. He washed the family car and earned **6** dollars. What is his weekly allowance if he ended with **14** dollars?

   E. $28   G. $13

   F. $20   H. $16

   Difficulty: Hard

6. Evergreen Bike Rental Shop charges a **17** dollar fixed fee plus **7** dollars an hour for renting a bike. Jessica paid **45** dollars to rent a bike. How many hours did she pay to have the bike checked out?

   A. 4   C. 7

   B. 6   D. 2

   Difficulty: Hard

7. Aubrianna spends $3\frac{1}{5}$ hours reading and spends $2\frac{4}{5}$ hours at the store. She spends $2\frac{3}{5}$ hours biking. How much less time does Aubrianna spend at the store compared to reading?

E. 6 hours

F. $\frac{2}{5}$ of an hour

G. $2\frac{3}{5}$ hours

H. $\frac{4}{5}$ of an hour

Difficulty: Moderate

8. Tangelo wants to complete $2\frac{4}{9}$ cross words today. Tangelo has already done $1\frac{6}{7}$ cross words. Tangelo also did $1\frac{3}{8}$ jumble puzzles. What fraction of crosswords does Tangelo have left to finish?

A. $\frac{28}{63}$

B. $\frac{37}{63}$

C. $\frac{54}{63}$

D. $\frac{91}{63}$

Difficulty: Hard

9. Ringo picked $2\frac{1}{4}$ buckets of apples, and Trey picked $2\frac{3}{7}$ buckets of apples. How many more buckets did Trey pick?

E. $\frac{12}{28}$

G. $\frac{19}{28}$

F. $\frac{7}{28}$

H. $\frac{5}{28}$

Difficulty: Hard

10. Brandon bought 12 boxes of cookies for his birthday party. He bought 48 cookies in all. Which equation shows how many cookies are in each box?

A. $48 - k = 12$

C. $12 \times k = 48$

B. $\frac{12}{k} = 48$

D. $12 + k = 48$

Difficulty: Hard

11. Jessie Boyd Elementary School filled 76 containers of recycled water bottles. If each container holds 64 bottles, how many total water bottles did the school recycle?

E. 2,864

G. 4,684

F. 5,864

H. 4,864

Difficulty: Moderate

1. Simpsonville Elementary School purchased **85** boxes of pencils for the upcoming school year. Each box contains **62** pencils. How many total pencils did the school purchase?

   A. 4,270   **C.** 2,635

   B. 5,270   **D.** 5,720

   Difficulty: **Moderate**

2. Francesca gained **5.54** pounds between her third and fourth birthdays. If she weighed **42.48** pounds when she turned **4**, how much did she weigh in pounds when she turned **3**?

   E. 36.94   **G.** 63.94

   F. 36.49   **H.** 48.02

   Difficulty: **Moderate**

3. Manny's Super Market bought **25** pounds of carrots for customers for the coming week. On the first day, customers bought **4.96** pounds of carrots and on the second day, they bought **5.63** pounds of carrots. How many pounds of carrots did Manny's Super Market have remaining for the week?

   A. 39.41   **C.** 14.41

   B. 25   **D.** 10.59

   Difficulty: **Hard**

4. Ella received **$2.37** for her weekly allowance. How much did she receive after three weeks?

   E. $11.70   **G.** $7.11

   F. $5.37   **H.** $8.37

   Difficulty: **Moderate**

5. The Central Valley School gymnasium purchased **53** packs of foam balls. If each pack of foam ball contains **24**, how many total foam balls did the school gymnasium purchase?

   A. 1,272   **C.** 29

   B. 77   **D.** 1,227

   Difficulty: **Moderate**

6. We drove **50** miles per hour to my grandmother's house without stopping. It took us **7** hours to get there. How many miles did we drive?

   E. 300   **G.** 357

   F. 350   **H.** 400

   Difficulty: **Moderate**

1. 56 is 7 times as many as _____

   A. 6   C. 8
   B. 7   D. 9

   Difficulty: Easy

2. 6 times as many as 6 is _____.

   E. 36   G. 56
   F. 42   H. 24

   Difficulty: Easy

3. 10 is _____ times as many as 5.

   A. 1   C. 3
   B. 4   D. 2

   Difficulty: Easy

4. 14 is 2 times as many as _____.

   E. 5   G. 7
   F. 8   H. 6

   Difficulty: Easy

5. 2 times as many as 9 is _____.

   A. 12   C. 20
   B. 18   D. 16

   Difficulty: Easy

6. Solve: 10 × (5 + 10)

   E. 1500   G. 50
   F. 15   H. 150

   Difficulty: Moderate

7. Solve: 3 × (42 ÷ 6)

   A. 21   C. 15
   B. 18   D. 24

   Difficulty: Moderate

8. Solve: (24 ÷ 3) × 5

   E. 35   G. 30
   F. 40   H. 25

   Difficulty: Moderate

9. Solve: (44 - 4) - 28

   A. 10   C. 12
   B. 14   D. 8

   Difficulty: Moderate

10. Solve: (2 + 5) × 10

    E. 60   G. 30
    F. 70   H. 100

    Difficulty: Moderate

11. A flower store has thirty-six roses and six tulips. How many times more roses did they have than tulips?

A. 4   C. 9
B. 8   D. 6

Difficulty: Moderate

12. Morris was playing a video game. It took him eight lives to beat the first world. It took eight times as many to beat the second world. How many lives did he use on the second world?

E. 56   G. 72
F. 64   H. 40

Difficulty: Moderate

13. In college, a science book costs seven times as much as a history book. If the history book costs two dollars, how much does the science book cost?

A. $10   C. $16
B. $12   D. $14

Difficulty: Moderate

14. Isaac was doing sit-ups. He did five times as many on Tuesday as he did on Monday. If he did forty sit-ups on Tuesday, how many did he do on Monday?

E. 8   G. 10
F. 6   H. 4

Difficulty: Moderate

15. For a fundraiser Jerry earned four dollars. Gretchen earned four times as much as Jerry earned. How much did Gretchen earn?

A. $12   C. $14
B. $10   D. $16

Difficulty: Moderate

16. Rewrite the number sentence using numerals and symbols: what is 1/7 of 1 less than 16?

E. $(16 - 1)$
F. $(16 - 7) \div 7$
G. $16 \div 7$
H. $(16 - 1) \div 7$

Difficulty: Moderate

1. Rewrite the number sentence using numerals and symbols: **8** divided by the sum of **9** and **3**

- **A.** $8 \div (9 - 3)$
- **B.** $8 \div (9 + 3)$
- **C.** $8 \div (9 \times 3)$
- **D.** $8 \div (9 \div 3)$

Difficulty: Moderate

2. Rewrite the number sentence using numerals and symbols: What is the quotient of **2** divided by **9** and then multiply **6**

- **E.** $6 \times (2 \times 9)$
- **F.** $6 - (2 \div 9)$
- **G.** $6 \times (2 \div 9)$
- **H.** $6 + (2 \div 9)$

Difficulty: Moderate

3. Rewrite the number sentence using numerals and symbols: Divide **22** by the difference between **18** and **7**

- **A.** $22 + (18 - 7)$
- **B.** $22 \div (18 - 7)$
- **C.** $22 \div (18 + 7)$
- **D.** $22 \times (18 - 7)$

Difficulty: Moderate

4. Rewrite the number sentence using numerals and symbols: Multiply **9** by the product of **4** and **9**

- **E.** $9 \times (4 \times 9)$
- **G.** $9 \times (4 + 9)$
- **F.** $9 + (4 \times 9)$
- **H.** $9 - (4 \times 9)$

Difficulty: Moderate

5. A donation center had filled up **35** small bins with canned food with each bin containing **42** cans. They plan to send the cans out to **6** food banks, but want to give each food bank the same number of cans. How many cans should they give to each food bank?

- **A.** 245
- **C.** 225
- **B.** 250
- **D.** 490

Difficulty: Hard

6. Madison's mother had **16** small photo albums filled with **21** photos in each. In order to save some space she bought **7** larger albums with each album having **20** pages. If she wanted to put all her pictures into the large albums, with the same number of pictures in each, how many pictures should be in each album?

- **E.** 96
- **G.** 48
- **F.** 24
- **H.** 46

Difficulty: Hard

7. An industrial machine made 1,629 cans of diet sodas and 6 times as many regular sodas over the course of 46 minutes. The regular sodas were then placed into 3 shipping boxes with each shipping box containing the same number of sodas. How many regular sodas were in each shipping box.

A. 1,629   C. 3,258

B. 1,638   D. 3,285

Difficulty: Hard

8. Marion developed a game for phones that he sold for $2. After the first week he discovered he had 5,456 downloads from girls and 4 times as many boys download the game. Of the boys who downloaded it he only had 1/8 who bought the full game. How many boys bought the full game?

E. 2,728   G. 5,456

F. 2,782   H. 5.465

Difficulty: Hard

9. A restaurant owner bought 3 boxes of disposable cups for $148, with each box containing 4,050 cups. If he wanted to divvy up the cups among his 9 restaurants, with each restaurant getting the same number of cups, how many cups should each store get?

A. 1, 530   C. 2,700

B. 3,902   D. 1,350

Difficulty: Hard

10. Which of the following is an equation that shows the relationship between the input and the output?

Input c	Output f
100	10
30	3
70	7
49	4
50	5

E. $c \times 10 = f$ G. $c + 10 = f$

F. $c \div 10 = f$ H. $c - 10 = f$

Difficulty: Moderate

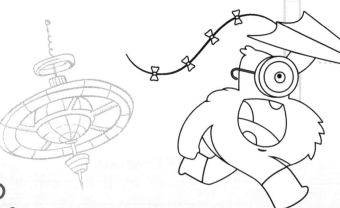

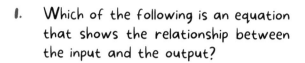

1. Which of the following is an equation that shows the relationship between the input and the output?

Input (q)	92	76	40	25
Output (p)	89	73	37	22

A. $q \times 3 = p$

B. $q \div 3 = p$

C. $q + 3 = p$

D. $q - 3 = p$

Difficulty: Hard

2. Which of the following is an equation that shows the relationship between the input and the output?

Input s	Output p
29	41
49	61
32	44
84	96
15	27

E. $s - 12 = p$

F. $s + 12 = p$

G. $s \times 12 = p$

H. $s \div 12 = p$

Difficulty: Hard

3. Select the choice that is a factor pair for the number 94.

A. 4 and 24

B. 6 and 16

C. 2 and 47

D. 5 and 19

Difficulty: Moderate

4. Select the choice that is a factor pair for the number 39.

E. 6 and 7

F. 3 and 13

G. 5 and 8

H. 7 and 6

Difficulty: Moderate

5. Which choice is a multiple of 2?

A. 29

B. 37

C. 23

D. 28

Difficulty: Moderate

6. Which choice is a multiple of 5?

E. 70

F. 59

G. 101

H. 103

Difficulty: Moderate

7. A toy store sold **93** video games in one day. If each game cost **20** dollars, how much money did they make?

   A. $1,860   C. $1,680

   B. $1,130   D. $1,068

   Difficulty: Moderate

8. If an industrial machine could make **44** erasers in a second, how many erasers would it have made in **69** seconds?

   E. 3,630   G. 3,360

   F. 3,036   H. 3,006

   Difficulty: Moderate

9. Marlene was placing her spare change into stacks. Each stack had **48** coins. If she had **51** stacks, how many coins did she have all together?

   A. 2,844   C. 2,800

   B. 2,484   D. 2,448

   Difficulty: Moderate

10. Germaine was building a LEGO tower. He built it **61** stories tall with **77** LEGOs on each story. How many LEGOs did he use total?

    E. 4,796   G. 4,900

    F. 4,967   H. 4,697

    Difficulty: Moderate

11. Determine which numbers best complete the pattern below:

I	II	21	31	41	?	?

    A. 51, 61   C. 31, 21

    B. 53, 63   D. 61, 71

    Difficulty: Moderate

12. Determine which numbers best complete the pattern below.

36	34	32	30	?	?

    E. 27, 23   G. 26, 28

    F. 24, 22   H. 28, 26

    Difficulty: Moderate

1. Determine which numbers best complete the pattern below.

| 11 | 13 | 15 | 17 | 19 | ? | ? |

A. 21, 23   C. 1, 15

B. 19, 24   D. 23, 25

Difficulty: Moderate

2. What is the third number in the pattern?

| 9 | 11 | ? | 15 | 17 | 19 |

E. 10   G. 9

F. 13   H. 14

Difficulty: Moderate

3. What is the fourth number in the pattern?

| 37 | 35 | 33 | ? | 29 |

A. 30   C. 31

B. 28   D. 32

Difficulty: Moderate

4. In a pattern the first number is a **5**. The second number is a **10**. The third is a **15**. Fourth is a **20**. If the pattern continues will the **23rd** number end in a **5** or a **0**?

E. 5   F. 0

Difficulty: Hard

5. In a pattern the first number is a **3**. The second number is a **6**. The third is a **9**. Fourth is a **12**. If the pattern continues what will be the **20th** number in the pattern?

A. 60   C. 57

B. 63   D. 54

Difficulty: Hard

6. A pattern starts with **9**. The second number is a **11**. The third is a **13**. Fourth is a **15** and fifth is **17**. Will the 11th number in the pattern be even or odd?

E. even   F. odd

Difficulty: Easy

7. Which of the following illustrates finding the quotient of **5** divided by **8** and then add **8**

A. $(5 \div 8) - 8$

B. $(5 \div 8) \times 8$

C. $(5 \div 8) + 8$

D. $(5 \div 8) \div 8$

Difficulty: Hard

8. Select the choice that is a factor pair for the number **8**.

E. 6 and 2   G. 2 and 4

F. 5 and 2   H. 3 and 2

Difficulty: Moderate

9. Select the choice that is a factor pair for the number **55**.

A. 8 and 7   **C.** 9 and 7

B. 7 and 8   **D.** 5 and 11

Difficulty: **Moderate**

10. A clown needed 18 balloons for a party he was going to, but the balloons only came in packs of **5**. How many packs of balloons would he need to buy?

E. 5   **G.** 4

F. 3   **H.** 2

Difficulty: **Hard**

11. A school had **17** students sign up for the trivia teams. If they wanted to have **5** teams, with the same number of students on each team, how many more students would need to sign up?

A. 2   **C.** 5

B. 4   **D.** 3

Difficulty: **Hard**

12. A restaurant needs to buy **22** new plates. If each box has **8** plates in it, how many boxes will they need to buy?

E. 3   **G.** 2

F. 4   **H.** 5

Difficulty: **Hard**

125

Geometry

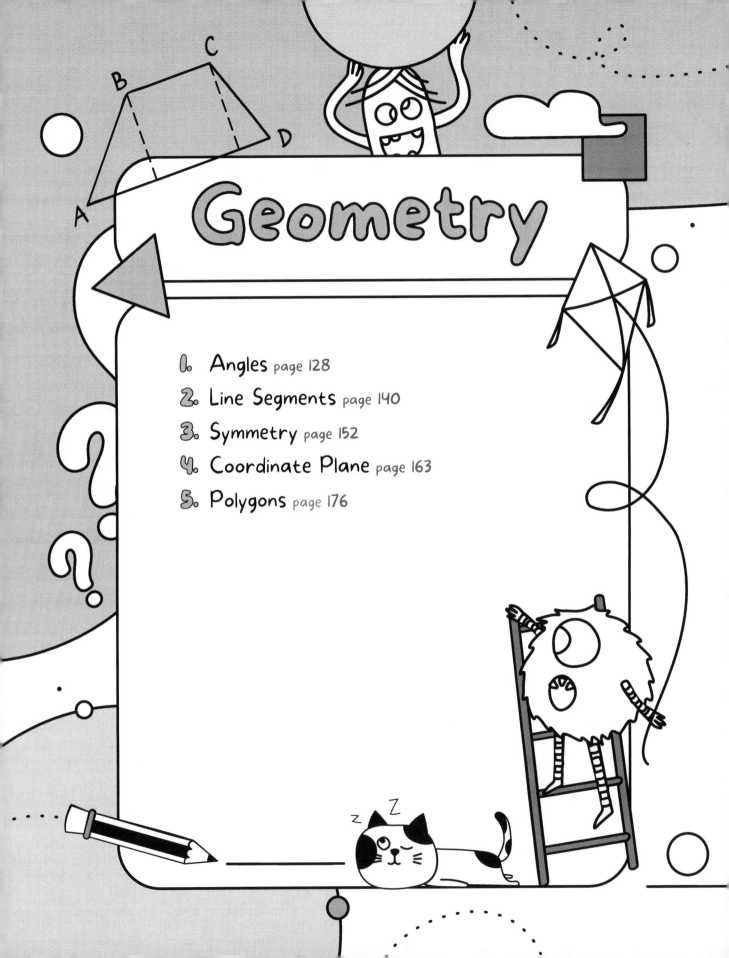

1. Is this angle acute, right, obtuse, or straight?

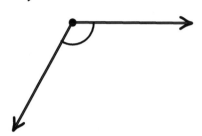

A. acute   C. right

B. obtuse   D. straight

Difficulty: Moderate

3. Is this angle acute, right, obtuse, or straight?

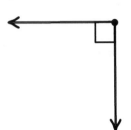

A. acute   C. right

B. obtuse   D. straight

Difficulty: Moderate

2. Is this angle acute, right, obtuse, or straight?

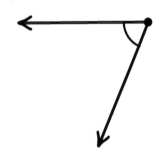

E. acute   G. right

F. obtuse   H. straight

Difficulty: Moderate

4. Is this angle acute, right, obtuse, or straight?

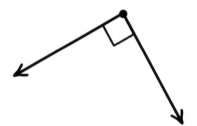

E. acute   G. right

F. obtuse   H. straight

Difficulty: Moderate

5. Is this angle acute, right, obtuse, or straight?

   A. acute   **C.** right

   B. obtuse   **D.** straight

   Difficulty: Moderate

6. Is an 89° angle acute, right, obtuse, or straight?

   E. acute   **G.** right

   F. obtuse   **H.** straight

   Difficulty: Easy

7. Is a 124° angle acute, right, obtuse, or straight?

   A. acute   **C.** right

   B. obtuse   **D.** straight

   Difficulty: Easy

8. Is a 180° angle acute, right, obtuse, or straight?

   E. acute   **G.** right

   F. obtuse   **H.** straight

   Difficulty: Easy

9. Is a 6° angle acute, right, obtuse, or straight?

   A. acute   **C.** right

   B. obtuse   **D.** straight

   Difficulty: Easy

10. Is a 90° angle acute, right, obtuse, or straight?

   E. acute   **G.** right

   F. obtuse   **H.** straight

   Difficulty: Easy

11. Is this angle acute, right, obtuse, or straight?

   A. acute   **C.** right

   B. obtuse   **D.** straight

   Difficulty: Moderate

12. Is this angle acute, right, obtuse, or straight?

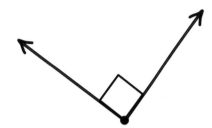

E. acute   **G.** right
F. obtuse   **H.** straight

Difficulty: Moderate

13. Is this angle acute, right, obtuse, or straight?

A. acute   **C.** right
B. obtuse   **D.** straight

Difficulty: Moderate

14. Is this angle acute, right, obtuse, or straight?

E. acute   **G.** right
F. obtuse   **H.** straight

Difficulty: Moderate

15. Is this angle acute, right, obtuse, or straight?

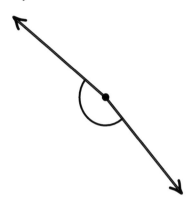

A. acute **C.** right

B. obtuse **D.** straight

Difficulty: Moderate

16. Which of the following is the type of angle labeled as number 1 in the figure below?

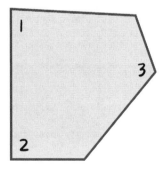

E. acute **G.** right

F. obtuse **H.** straight

Difficulty: Hard

17. Which of the following is the type of angle labeled as number **3** in the figure below?

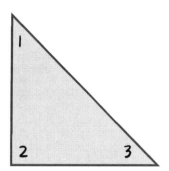

A. acute **C.** right

B. obtuse **D.** straight

Difficulty: Hard

1. Which of the following is the type of angle labeled as number **7** in the figure below?

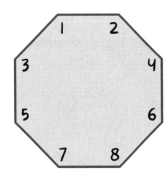

E. acute   **G.** right

F. obtuse   **H.** straight

Difficulty: Hard

3. Which of the following is the type of angle as labeled number **2** in the figure below?

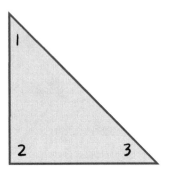

E. acute   **G.** right

F. obtuse   **H.** straight

Difficulty: Hard

2. Which of the following is the type of angle labeled as number **2** in the figure below?

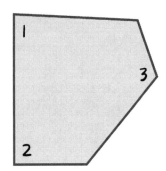

A. acute   **C.** right

B. obtuse   **D.** straight

Difficulty: Hard

4. Which choice best represents ∠KLM?

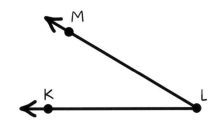

A. 180°   **C.** 115°

B. 92°   **D.** 31°

Difficulty: Hard

5. Which choice best represents ∠KLM?

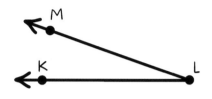

E. 99°   G. 169°

F. 19°   H. 66°

Difficulty: Hard

6. Which choice best represents ∠ABC?

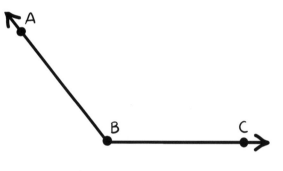

A. 20°   C. 129°

B. 47°   D. 175°

Difficulty: Hard

7. Which choice best represents ∠ABC?

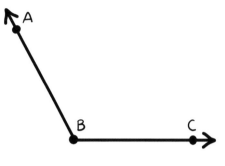

E. 119°   G. 169°

F. 98°   H. 9°

Difficulty: Hard

8. Which choice best represents ∠ABC?

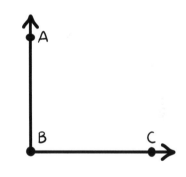

A. 90°   C. 3°

B. 151°   D. 54°

Difficulty: Hard

9. Is this angle greater than, equal to, less than a right angle, or is it not an angle?

E. greater than
F. less than
G. equal to
H. is not an angle

Difficulty: Moderate

11. Is this angle greater than, equal to, less than a right angle, or is it not an angle?

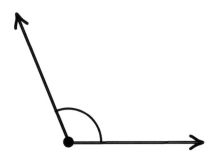

E. greater than
F. less than
G. equal to
H. is not an angle

Difficulty: Moderate

10. Is this angle greater than, equal to, less than a right angle, or is it not an angle?

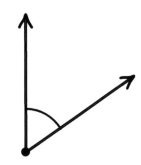

A. greater than
B. less than
C. equal to
D. is not an angle

Difficulty: Moderate

12. Is this angle greater than, equal to, less than a right angle, or is it not an angle?

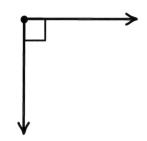

A. greater than
B. less than
C. equal to
D. is not an angle

Difficulty: Moderate

13. Is this angle greater than, equal to, less than a right angle, or is it not an angle?

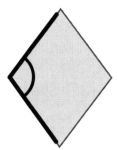

E. greater than
F. less than
G. equal to
H. is not an angle

Difficulty: Moderate

15. Is this angle greater than, equal to, less than a right angle, or is it not an angle?

E. greater than
F. less than
G. equal to
H. is not an angle

Difficulty: Moderate

14. Is this angle greater than, equal to, less than a right angle, or is it not an angle?

A. greater than
B. less than
C. equal to
D. is not an angle

Difficulty: Moderate

16. Is this angle greater than, equal to, less than a right angle, or is it not an angle?

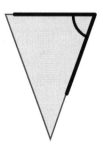

A. greater than
B. less than
C. equal to
D. is not an angle

Difficulty: Moderate

1. Is this angle greater than, equal to, less than a right angle, or is it not an angle?

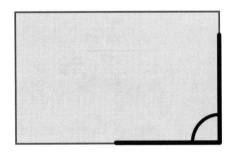

E. greater than
F. less than
G. equal to
H. is not an angle

Difficulty: Moderate

2. Is this angle greater than, equal to, less than a right angle, or is it not an angle?

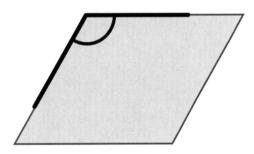

A. greater than
B. less than
C. equal to
D. is not an angle

Difficulty: Moderate

3. Is this angle acute, right, obtuse, or straight?

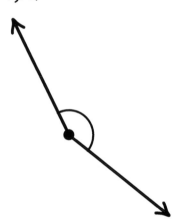

E. acute   **G.** obtuse
F. right   **H.** straight

Difficulty: Moderate

4. Is this angle acute, right, obtuse, or straight?

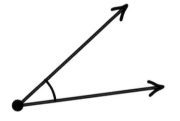

A. acute   **C.** obtuse
B. right   **D.** straight

Difficulty: Moderate

5. Is this angle acute, right, obtuse, or straight?

- **E.** acute
- **F.** right
- **G.** obtuse
- **H.** straight

Difficulty: Moderate

6. Is this angle acute, right, obtuse, or straight?

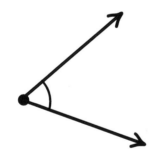

- **A.** acute
- **B.** right
- **C.** obtuse
- **D.** straight

Difficulty: Moderate

7. Is this angle acute, right, obtuse, or straight?

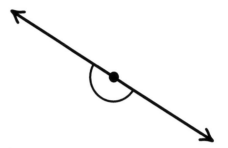

- **E.** acute
- **F.** right
- **G.** obtuse
- **H.** straight

Difficulty: Moderate

8. Two rays meeting at ends form _____ .

- **A.** a square
- **B.** an angle
- **C.** a rectangle
- **D.** a triangle

Difficulty: Moderate

9. Which of the following angle measures could represent an acute angle?

- **E.** 94°
- **F.** 90°
- **G.** 125°
- **H.** 68°

Difficulty: Moderate

10. Which of the following angle measures could represent an obtuse angle?

A. 180° **C.** 88°

B. 29° **D.** 161°

Difficulty: Moderate

11. Which of the following angle measures could represent a straight angle?

E. 180° **G.** 125°

F. 90° **H.** 68°

Difficulty: Moderate

12. Which of the following angle measures could represent a right angle?

A. 180° **C.** 90°

B. 29° **D.** 161°

Difficulty: Moderate

13. What type of angle is angle number 4?

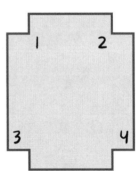

A. acute **C.** right

B. obtuse **D.** straight

Difficulty: Hard

14. What type of angle is angle number 1?

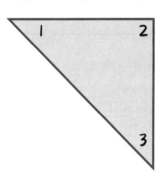

E. acute **G.** right

F. obtuse **H.** straight

Difficulty: Hard

15. What type of angle is angle number 3?

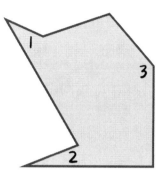

A. acute   C. right
B. obtuse   D. straight

Difficulty: Hard

16. What type of angle is angle number 2?

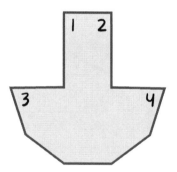

E. acute   G. right
F. obtuse   H. straight

Difficulty: Hard

17. What type of angle is angle number 2?

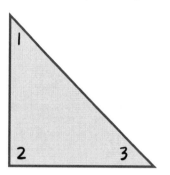

A. acute   C. right
B. obtuse   D. straight

Difficulty: Hard

1. Identify the following:

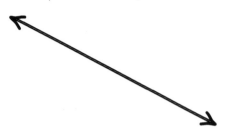

A. line
B. ray
C. line segment
D. point

Difficulty: Easy

2. Identify the following:

E. line
F. ray
G. line segment
H. point

Difficulty: Easy

3. Identify the following:

A. line
B. ray
C. line segment
D. point

Difficulty: Easy

4. Identify the following:

E. line
F. ray
G. line segment
H. point

Difficulty: Easy

5. Identify the following:

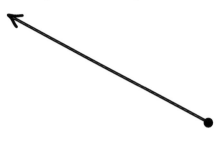

A. line
B. ray
C. line segment
D. point

Difficulty: Easy

7. Identify the following:

A. line
B. ray
C. line segment
D. point

Difficulty: Easy

6. Identify the following:

E. line
F. ray
G. line segment
H. point

Difficulty: Easy

8. Identify the following:

E. line
F. ray
G. line segment
H. point

Difficulty: Easy

9. Identify the following:

A. line
B. ray
C. line segment
D. point

Difficulty: Easy

10. In the triangular prism shown below, which lines are parallel?

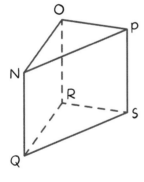

E. $\overleftrightarrow{OR}$ and $\overleftrightarrow{PS}$
F. $\overleftrightarrow{OR}$ and $\overleftrightarrow{NO}$
G. $\overleftrightarrow{NP}$ and $\overleftrightarrow{NQ}$
H. $\overleftrightarrow{NP}$ and $\overleftrightarrow{NO}$

Difficulty: Hard

11. In the cube shown below, which lines are parallel?

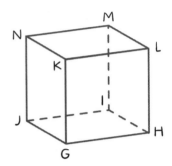

A. $\overleftrightarrow{HI}$ and $\overleftrightarrow{IM}$
B. $\overleftrightarrow{HL}$ and $\overleftrightarrow{JN}$
C. $\overleftrightarrow{GK}$ and $\overleftrightarrow{IJ}$
D. $\overleftrightarrow{NM}$ and $\overleftrightarrow{JN}$

Difficulty: Hard

12. In the rectangular prism shown below, which lines are parallel?

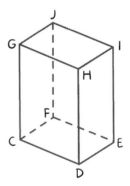

E. $\overleftrightarrow{HI}$ and $\overleftrightarrow{DH}$
F. $\overleftrightarrow{FJ}$ and $\overleftrightarrow{GH}$
G. $\overleftrightarrow{DH}$ and $\overleftrightarrow{EI}$
H. $\overleftrightarrow{HI}$ and $\overleftrightarrow{DC}$

Difficulty: Hard

13. In the triangular prism shown below, which lines are parallel?

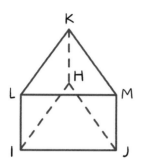

A. $\overline{HJ}$ and $\overleftrightarrow{KM}$
B. $\overline{HJ}$ and $\overline{JM}$
C. $\overleftrightarrow{KL}$ and $\overleftrightarrow{JM}$
D. $\overleftrightarrow{HJ}$ and $\overleftrightarrow{JM}$

Difficulty: Hard

14. These lines are _____ .

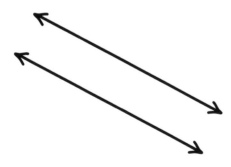

E. perpendicular
F. parallel
G. rays
H. intersecting

Difficulty: Easy

15. These lines _____ .

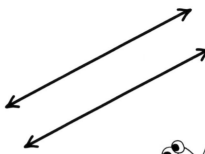

A. perpendicular
B. parallel
C. rays
D. intersecting

Difficulty: Easy

16. These lines are _____ .

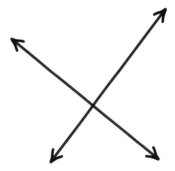

E. perpendicular
F. parallel
G. rays
H. intersecting

Difficulty: Moderate

1. These lines are _____ ?

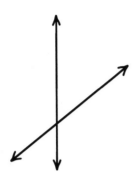

- **A.** perpendicular
- **B.** parallel
- **C.** rays
- **D.** intersecting

Difficulty: Easy

2. In the triangular prism shown below, which lines are parallel?

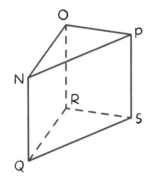

- **E.** $\overleftrightarrow{OR}$ and $\overleftrightarrow{PN}$
- **F.** $\overleftrightarrow{OR}$ and $\overleftrightarrow{NO}$
- **G.** $\overleftrightarrow{NP}$ and $\overleftrightarrow{SQ}$
- **H.** $\overleftrightarrow{OR}$ and $\overleftrightarrow{OP}$

Difficulty: Hard

3. In the cube shown below, which lines are parallel?

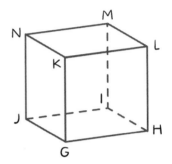

- **A.** $\overleftrightarrow{HI}$ and $\overleftrightarrow{IM}$
- **B.** $\overleftrightarrow{HL}$ and $\overleftrightarrow{JN}$
- **C.** $\overleftrightarrow{GK}$ and $\overleftrightarrow{IJ}$
- **D.** $\overleftrightarrow{HI}$ and $\overleftrightarrow{IJ}$

Difficulty: Hard

4. In the rectangular prism shown below, which lines are parallel?

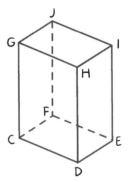

- **E.** $\overleftrightarrow{HI}$ and $\overleftrightarrow{DH}$
- **F.** $\overleftrightarrow{FJ}$ and $\overleftrightarrow{GH}$
- **G.** $\overleftrightarrow{DH}$ and $\overleftrightarrow{EI}$
- **H.** $\overleftrightarrow{DH}$ and $\overleftrightarrow{ED}$

Difficulty: Hard

5. In the triangular prism shown below, which lines are parallel?

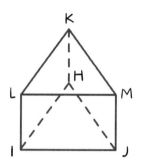

A. $\overleftrightarrow{HJ}$ and $\overleftrightarrow{KM}$
B. $\overleftrightarrow{HJ}$ and $\overleftrightarrow{JM}$
C. $\overleftrightarrow{KL}$ and $\overleftrightarrow{JM}$
D. $\overleftrightarrow{HJ}$ and $\overleftrightarrow{JI}$

Difficulty: Hard

6. How many pairs of opposite sides are parallel?

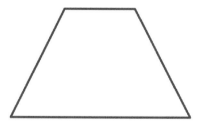

E. 1 pair   **G.** 4 pairs
F. 2 pairs   **H.** none

Difficulty: Hard

7. How many pairs of opposite sides are parallel?

A. 1 pair   **C.** 4 pairs
B. 2 pairs   **D.** no pairs

Difficulty: Hard

8. How many pairs of opposite sides are parallel?

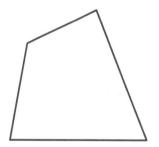

E. 1 pair   **G.** 4 pairs
F. 2 pairs   **H.** no pairs

Difficulty: Hard

9. How many pairs of opposite sides are parallel?

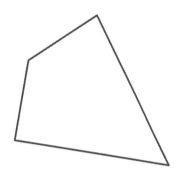

A. 1 pair   C. 4 pairs

B. 2 pairs   D. no pairs

Difficulty: Hard

10. What is this?

E. point
F. line segment
G. line
H. ray

Difficulty: Easy

11. What is this?

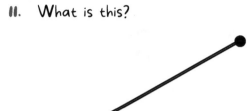

A. ray
B. line
C. point
D. line segment

Difficulty: Easy

12. What is the name of this figure?

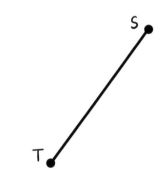

E. $\overrightarrow{ST}$ G. $\overline{ST}$

F. $\overleftrightarrow{ST}$ H. $\overline{ST}$

Difficulty: Moderate

13. What is the name of this figure?

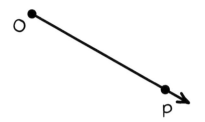

A. $\overline{OP}$ **C.** $\overrightarrow{OP}$

B. $\overrightarrow{OP}$ **D.** $\overleftrightarrow{OP}$

Difficulty: Moderate

14. What is the name of this figure?

E. $\overrightarrow{OP}$ **G.** $\overleftrightarrow{OP}$

F. $\overrightarrow{OP}$ **H.** $\overline{OP}$

Difficulty: Moderate

15. Which of the figures below shows Acute ∠ BDE?

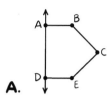
A.

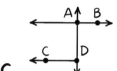
C.

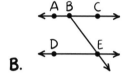
B.

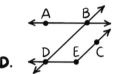
D.

Difficulty: Moderate

16. Which of the figures below shows Right ∠ ADE?

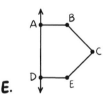
E.

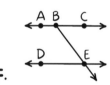
G.

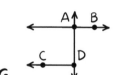
F.

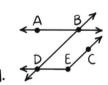
H.

Difficulty: Moderate

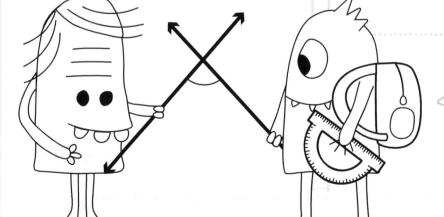

1. These lines are _____ .

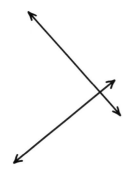

- **A.** perpendicular
- **B.** parallel
- **C.** rays
- **D.** segments

Difficulty: Easy

2. These lines are _____ .

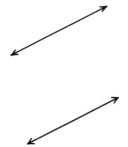

- **E.** perpendicular
- **F.** parallel
- **G.** rays
- **H.** intersecting

Difficulty: Easy

3. These lines are _____ .

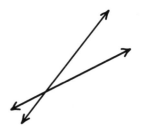

- **A.** perpendicular
- **B.** parallel
- **C.** rays
- **D.** intersecting

Difficulty: Easy

For questions 4 - 6 , use the image below:

Pine St
Stephenson St
School St
Queen St
Johnston St
Oak St
Oak St
Church St
Center St
Main St

4. Which of the following streets is parallel to Oak Street?

   E. School St.
   F. Center St.
   G. Church St.
   H. Queen St.

   Difficulty: Hard

5. Oak St. and Johnston Streets are _____ .

   A. rays
   B. parallel
   C. perpendicular
   D. points

   Difficulty: Hard

6. Main Street and Johnston Street are _____ .

   E. intersecting
   F. parallel
   G. perpendicular
   H. points

   Difficulty: Hard

7. If two lines are parallel, they are _____ .

   A. different distances apart.
   B. perpendicular to each other.
   C. the same distance apart.
   D. intersecting each other.

   Difficulty: Moderate

8. Lines that meet or cross each other to form right angles are called _____ lines.

   E. parallel
   F. intersecting
   G. ray
   H. perpendicular

   Difficulty: Moderate

9. Lines that meet or cross each other are called _____ lines.

   A. parallel
   B. intersecting
   C. ray
   D. perpendicular

   Difficulty: Moderate

10. A _____ is a straight set of points that extend in opposite directions without ending.

    E. point
    F. ray
    G. line segment
    H. line

    Difficulty: Moderate

11. A _____ is a part of a line that has one endpoint and extends in one direction without ending.

    A. point
    B. ray
    C. line segment
    D. line

    Difficulty: Moderate

12. A _____ is a part of a line between two endpoints.

    E. point
    F. ray
    G. line segment
    H. line

    Difficulty: Moderate

For numbers 13 – 18, use the following figure:

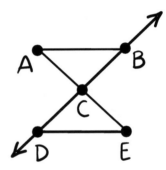

13. Which of the following is a line?

    A. CB   C. EC
    B. CA   D. DB

    Difficulty: Hard

14. Which of the following is ray?

    E. AB   **G.** CA

    F. CD   **H.** BD

Difficulty: Moderate

15. Which of the following is a line segment?

    A. AB   **C.** CB

    B. CD   **D.** DB

Difficulty: Moderate

16. Which of the following is a parallel line?

    E. there are none

    F. DB

    G. CB

    H. CD

Difficulty: Moderate

17. Which of the following is a perpendicular line?

    A. there are none

    B. AB

    C. CD

    D. DB

Difficulty: Moderate

18. Which of the following is an intersecting line?

    E. AB

    F. CB

    G. CE

    H. there are none

Difficulty: Moderate

1. The dotted line in the image below is a line of symmetry.

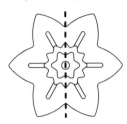

A. True   **B.** False

Difficulty: Easy

2. The dotted line in the image below is a line of symmetry.

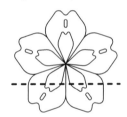

C. True   **D.** False

Difficulty: Easy

3. How many lines of symmetry does this polygon have?

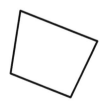

E. 3   **G.** 1
F. 2   **H.** 0

Difficulty: Hard

4. How many lines of symmetry does this polygon have?

A. 2   **C.** 1
B. 4   **D.** 6

Difficulty: Moderate

5. How many lines of symmetry does this figure have?

E. 0   **G.** 1
F. 2   **H.** 4

Difficulty: Hard

6. How many lines of symmetry does this figure have?

A. 0   **C.** 2
B. 1   **D.** 4

Difficulty: Hard

---

7. How many lines of symmetry does this figure have?

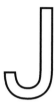

E. 2   G. 0

F. 1   H. 5

Difficulty: Hard

---

8. How many lines of symmetry does this polygon have?

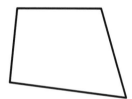

A. 0   C. 4

B. 2   D. 1

Difficulty: Hard

---

9. How many lines of symmetry does this shape have?

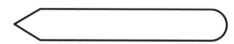

E. 0   G. 2

F. 1   H. 3

Difficulty: Hard

---

10. How many lines of symmetry does this polygon have?

A. 0   C. 2

B. 4   D. 1

Difficulty:

---

11. The image below has _____ symmetry.

E. rotational   G. 1 line of

F. no   H. 2 lines of

Difficulty: Moderate

1. The image below has _____ symmetry.

A. 10 lines of
B. only 1 line of symmetry
C. no
D. rotational

Difficulty: **Moderate**

2. How many lines of symmetry does this polygon have?

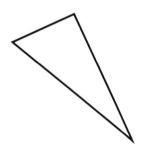

E. 1   G. 2
F. 3   H. 0

Difficulty: **Hard**

3. The image below has _____ symmetry.

A. rotational
B. only 1 line of
C. only 2 lines of
D. no

Difficulty: **Moderate**

4. The image below has _____ symmetry.

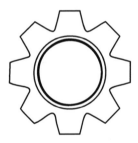

E. only 1 line of
F. rotational
G. no
H. only 2 lines of

Difficulty: **Moderate**

Geometry
1.2 Symmetry

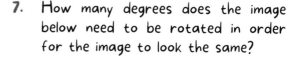

5. The image below has _____ symmetry.

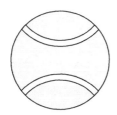

- **A.** no
- **B.** only 2 lines of
- **C.** only 1 line of
- **D.** rotational

Difficulty: Moderate

6. The image below has _____ symmetry.

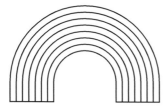

- **E.** only 1 line of
- **F.** only 2 lines of
- **G.** no
- **H.** rotational

Difficulty: Moderate

7. How many degrees does the image below need to be rotated in order for the image to look the same?

- **A.** 48°
- **C.** 45°
- **B.** 60°
- **D.** 190°

Difficulty: Hard

8. How many degrees does the image below need to be rotated in order for the image to look the same?

- **E.** 60°
- **G.** 270°
- **F.** 90°
- **H.** 45°

Difficulty: Moderate

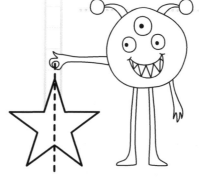

155

9. How many degrees does the image below need to be rotated in order for the image to look the same?

A. 20°   **C.** 90°

B. 160°   **D.** 50°

Difficulty: Moderate

10. How many degrees does the image below need to be rotated in order for the image to look the same?

E. 90°   **G.** 20°

F. 45°   **H.** 60°

Difficulty: Moderate

11. How many degrees does the image below need to be rotated in order for the image to look the same?

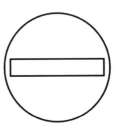

A. 90°   **C.** 30°

B. 45°   **D.** 180°

Difficulty: Moderate

12. How many degrees does the image below need to be rotated in order for the image to look the same?

E. 100°   **G.** 45°

F. 30°   **H.** 25°

Difficulty: Hard

1. How many degrees does the image below need to be rotated in order for the image to look the same?

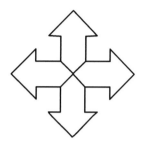

E. 60°

G. 90°

F. 200°

H. 45°

Difficulty: Moderate

2. How many degrees does the image below need to be rotated in order for the image to look the same?

A. 45°

C. 210°

B. 60°

D. 30°

Difficulty: Moderate

3. How many lines of symmetry does this shape have?

E. 1

G. 3

F. 2

H. 0

Difficulty: Hard

4. How many lines of symmetry does this shape have?

A. 1

C. 3

B. 2

D. 5

Difficulty: Hard

5. How many lines of symmetry does this shape have?

E. 1

G. 3

F. 2

H. 0

Difficulty: Hard

6. How many lines of symmetry does this shape have?

A. 4   C. 0

B. 2   D. 3

Difficulty: Hard

7. How many lines of symmetry does this shape have?

E. 1   G. 3

F. 2   H. 0

Difficulty: Hard

8. How many lines of symmetry does the figure below have?

A. 8   C. 4

B. 6   D. 2

Difficulty: Hard

9. How many lines of symmetry does the figure below have?

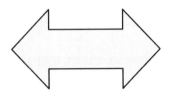

E. 1   G. 0

F. 2   H. 4

Difficulty: Hard

10. How many lines of symmetry does the figure below have?

A. 1   C. 3

B. 2   D. 4

Difficulty: Hard

11. How many lines of symmetry does the figure below have?

E. 3   G. 9

F. 6   H. 5

Difficulty: Hard

12. The image below has _____ symmetry.

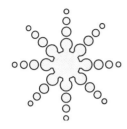

- **A.** rotational
- **B.** only 1 line of
- **C.** only 2 lines of
- **D.** no

Difficulty: Moderate

13. The image below has _____ symmetry.

- **E.** no
- **F.** rotational
- **G.** only 1 line of
- **H.** only 2 lines of

Difficulty: Moderate

14. The image below has _____ symmetry.

- **A.** rotational
- **B.** only 1 line of
- **C.** only 2 lines of
- **D.** no

Difficulty: Moderate

15. The image below has _____ symmetry.

- **E.** no
- **F.** rotational
- **G.** only 1 line of
- **H.** only 2 lines of

Difficulty: Moderate

1. One line of symmetry is shown on the figure below. How many other lines of symmetry does this figure have?

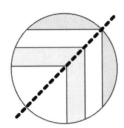

E. 0   G. 2

F. 1   H. 4

Difficulty: Moderate

2. The 4th grade class had to draw symmetrical figures. Bruce drew figure A shown below and drew the dotted line through the figure. Bruce said, "The dotted line is a line of symmetry." Armand drew figure B, Etienne drew figure C, and Pamela drew figure D. Whose figure shows a line of symmetry on their shape?

A   B   C   D

A. Bruce   C. Etienne

B. Armand   D. Pamela

Difficulty: Hard

3. Choose the figure for which both parts match when folded on the line.

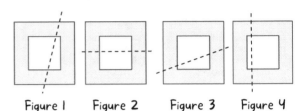

Figure 1   Figure 2   Figure 3   Figure 4

E. Figure 1   G. Figure 4

F. Figure 2   H. Figure 3

Difficulty: Hard

4. Identify the figure for which both parts match when folded on the line.

Figure 1   Figure 2   Figure 3   Figure 4

A. Figure 4   C. Figure 1

B. Figure 3   D. Figure 2

Difficulty: Hard

5. Identify the figure for which both parts match when folded on the line.

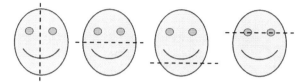

Figure 1   Figure 2   Figure 3   Figure 4

E. Figure 4   **G.** Figure 1

F. Figure 2   **H.** Figure 3

Difficulty: Hard

6. Identify the figure where the dotted line divides the figure into two symmetrical halves.

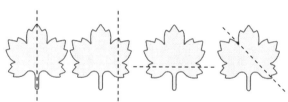

Figure 1   Figure 2   Figure 3   Figure 4

A. Figure 1   **C.** Figure 3

B. Figure 4   **D.** Figure 2

Difficulty: Hard

7. Identify the figure where the dotted line divides the figure into two symmetrical halves.

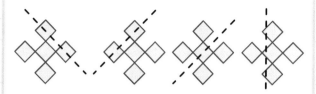

Figure 1   Figure 2   Figure 3   Figure 4

E. Figure 2   **G.** Figure 1

F. Figure 3   **H.** Figure 4

Difficulty: Hard

8. Which of the figures has both vertical and horizontal line of symmetry?

Figure 1   Figure 2

Figure 3   Figure 4

A. Figure 3   **C.** Figure 1

B. Figure 4   **D.** Figure 2

Difficulty: Hard

9. Which figure has more than one line of symmetry?

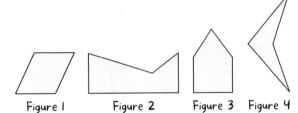

Figure 1   Figure 2   Figure 3   Figure 4

E. Figure 4   G. Figure 2
F. Figure 1   H. Figure 3

Difficulty: Hard

10. Which figure has a line of symmetry?

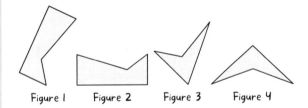

Figure 1   Figure 2   Figure 3   Figure 4

A. Figure 3   C. Figure 2
B. Figure 1   D. Figure 4

Difficulty: Easy

11. Count the number of lines of symmetry to the figure. How many are there?

E. 8   G. 6
F. 3   H. 10

Difficulty: Hard

12. How many lines of symmetry does the figure have?

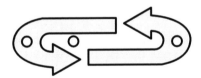

A. 1   C. 2
B. 3   D. 0

Difficulty: Moderate

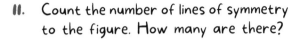

For questions 1 - 4, use the following graph:

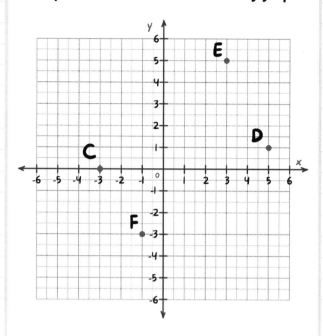

1. The x-coordinate of point D is:

A. 1   C. -5

B. 5   D. -1

Difficulty: Easy

2. The y-coordinate of point F is:

E. -1   G. 3

F. -3   H. 1

Difficulty: Easy

3. The x-coordinate of point E is:

A. 5   C. -3

B. 3   D. -5

Difficulty: Easy

4. The y-coordinate of point C is:

E. 0   G. -3

F. 3   H. 1

Difficulty: Easy

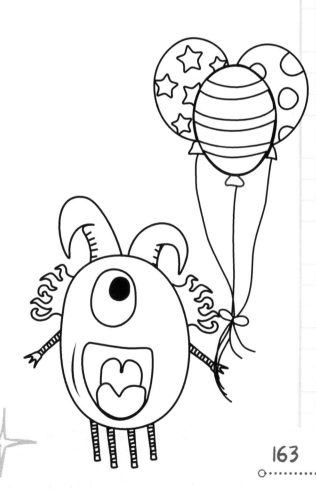

For questions 5 – 8, use the following graph:

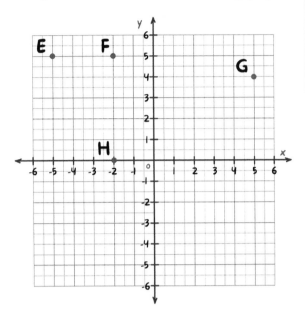

5. The coordinates of point H are:

    A. (-2, 0)   **C.** (0, -2)

    B. (2, 0)   **D.** (0, 0)

Difficulty: Easy

6. The coordinates of point E are:

    E. (5, -5)   **G.** (-5, 0)

    F. (-5, 5)   **H.** (0, -5)

Difficulty: Moderate

7. The coordinates of point G are:

    A. (4, 5)   **C.** (5, 4)

    B. (5, 0)   **D.** (0, 5)

Difficulty: Moderate

8. The coordinates of point F are:

    E. (5, -2)   **G.** (0, -5)

    F. (-2, 5)   **H.** (-5, 0)

Difficulty: Moderate

9. What are the coordinates of point R?

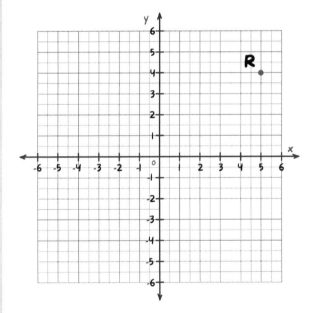

    A. (5, -5)   **C.** (-4, 5)

    B. (5, 4)   **D.** (-5, 5)

Difficulty: Hard

1. What are the coordinates of point A?

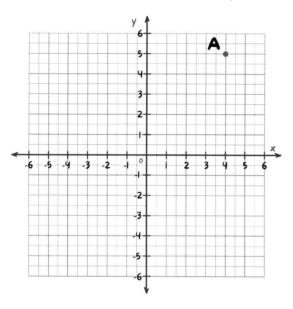

A. (4, 5)
B. (5, 4)
C. (5, 5)
D. (-5, 5)

Difficulty: Hard

2. What are the coordinates of point T?

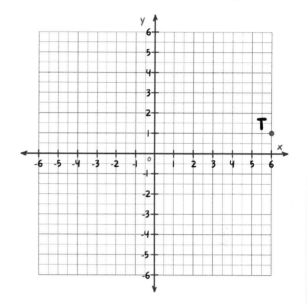

E. (5, 1)
F. (6, 4)
G. (6, 1)
H. (1, 5)

Difficulty: Hard

Use the graph below for numbers 3 – 6:

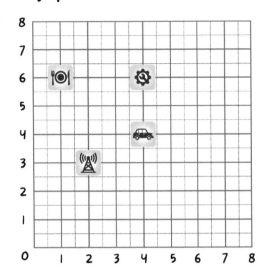

🚗 car delership

📡 radio tower

⚙️ hardware store

🍽️ restaurant

3. Where is the restaurant?

   A. (2, 3)
   B. (4, 4)
   C. (6, 4)
   D. (1, 6)

   Difficulty: Moderate

4. Where is the car dealership?

   E. (2, 3)
   F. (4, 4)
   G. (6, 4)
   H. (1, 6)

   Difficulty: Moderate

5. Where is the radio tower?

   A. (2, 3)
   B. (4, 4)
   C. (6, 4)
   D. (1, 6)

   Difficulty: Moderate

6. Where is the hardware store?

   E. (4, 6)
   F. (4, 4)
   G. (6, 4)
   H. (1, 6)

   Difficulty: Moderate

For numbers 1 – 6, use the graph below:

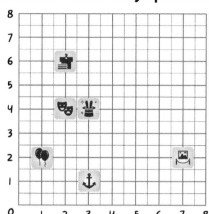

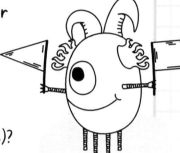

- 🎈 party supply store
- 🏭 dry cleaners
- ⚓ harbor
- 🎇 magic shop
- 🖼 art gallery
- 🎭 theater

1. What is at (2, 4)?

   A. party supply store
   B. theater
   C. harbor
   D. magic shop

   Difficulty: Moderate

2. What is at (3, 1)?

   E. party supply store
   F. dry cleaners
   G. harbor
   H. magic shop

   Difficulty: Moderate

3. What is at (2, 6)?

   A. party supply store
   B. dry cleaners
   C. harbor
   D. magic shop

   Difficulty: Moderate

4. What is at (1, 2)?

   E. party supply store
   F. dry cleaners
   G. harbor
   H. magic shop

   Difficulty: Moderate

5. What is at (7, 2)?

   A. art gallery   **C.** magic shop
   B. harbor   **D.** theater

   Difficulty: Moderate

6. What is at (3, 4)?

   E. party supply store
   F. dry cleaners
   G. harbor
   H. magic shop

   Difficulty: Moderate

7. You start at **(2, 5)** which is where the post office is and you need to get to the grocery store. You move left 1 unit to get to the grocery store. Where do you end?

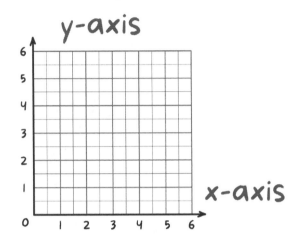

y-axis

x-axis

A. (5, 1)
B. (5, 5)
C. (1, 5)
D. (-5, -1)

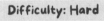

Difficulty: Hard

8. You start at the park which is at the coordinates **(2, 3)**. You move right **3** units to get to the ball field. Where do you end?

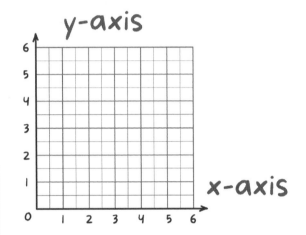

y-axis

x-axis

E. (-5, 3)
F. (5, -3)
G. (5, 3)
H. (3, 5)

Difficulty: Hard

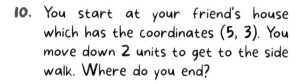

9. You start at (4, 3) which are the coordinates for your house and you want to get to the outside storage building to get your bike. You move up 1 unit. What are the coordinates of where you end?

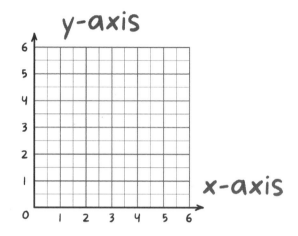

A. (0, 4)
B. (-4, 4)
C. (4, -4)
D. (4, 4)

Difficulty: Hard

10. You start at your friend's house which has the coordinates (5, 3). You move down 2 units to get to the side walk. Where do you end?

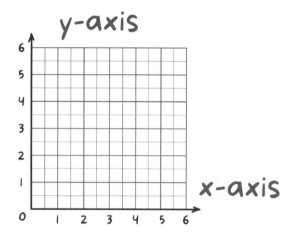

E. (1, 5)
F. (-5, 1)
G. (5, -1)
H. (5, 1)

Difficulty: Hard

1. Your mother started at (2, 4), which are the coordinates of the shopping center. She has to move to the right 1 unit to get to her car. Where does she end? _____

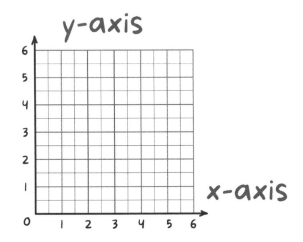

E. (4, 3)
F. (3, 4)
G. (-3, 4)
H. (3, -4)

Difficulty: Hard

2. Houston started at the coordinates of (1, 4) and needed to get to the baseball diamond. He needs to move up 2 units. Where does he end?

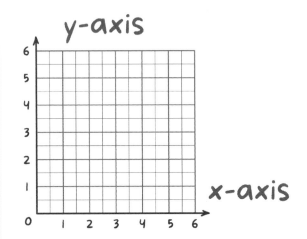

A. (1, 6)
B. (-1, 6)
C. (6, -1)
D. (6, 1)

Difficulty: Hard

3. Lindsay started at **(6, 5)**, the coordinates for her favorite toy store. She moves down 1 unit to get to the ice cream parlor. Where does she end?

y-axis

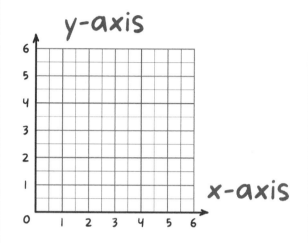

x-axis

E. (4, 6)
F. (-4, 6)
G. (6, 4)
H. (6, -4)

Difficulty: Hard

4. What are the coordinates of the star?

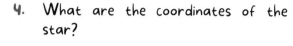

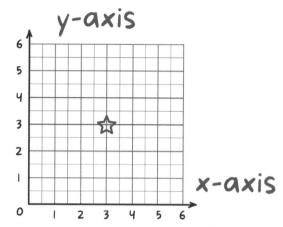

A. (-3, 3)   C. (3, -3)
B. (3, 3)   D. (0, 3)

Difficulty: Moderate

171

5. What are the coordinates of the diamond?

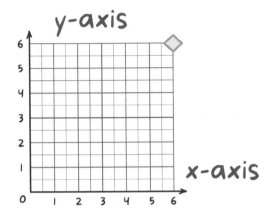

E. (5, 5)   G. (5, 6)

F. (6,6)   H. (6, 5)

Difficulty: Moderate

7. What are the coordinates of the pentagon?

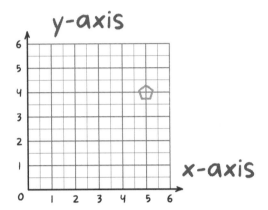

E. (4, 5)   G. (-5, 4)

F. (5, 4)   H. (5, -4)

Difficulty: Moderate

6. What are the coordinates of the heart?

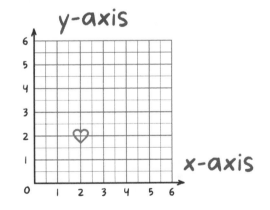

A. (1, 3)   C. (3, 3)

B. (2, 2)   D. (2, 3)

Difficulty: Moderate

8. What are the coordinates of the triangle?

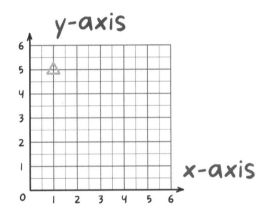

A. (5, 1)   C. (1, 5)

B. (5, -1)   D. (-1, 5)

Difficulty: Moderate

For numbers 9 - 12, use the following coordinate plane:

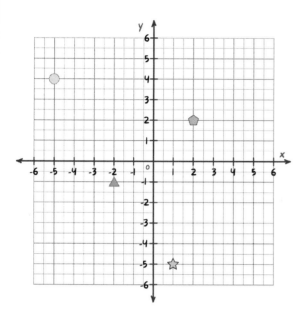

9. What shape is in quadrant II ?

    E.   star

    F.   triangle

    G.   pentagon

    H.   circle

Difficulty: Moderate

10. What shape is in quadrant IV ?

    A.   triangle

    B.   star

    C.   circle

    D.   pentagon

Difficulty: Moderate

11. What shape is in quadrant I ?

    E.   pentagon

    F.   star

    G.   triangle

    H.   circle

Difficulty: Moderate

12. What shape is in quadrant III ?

    A.   star

    B.   circle

    C.   triangle

    D.   pentagon

Difficulty: Moderate

For numbers 1 - 4, use the following coordinate plane:

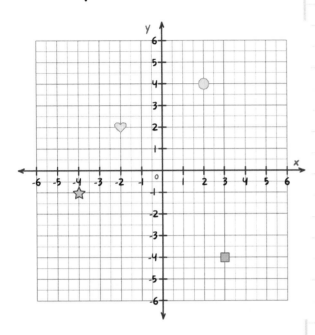

1. What shape is in quadrant IV ?

   E. star
   F. square
   G. heart
   H. circle

Difficulty: Moderate

2. What shape is in quadrant I ?

   A. circle
   B. star
   C. square
   D. heart

Difficulty: Moderate

3. What shape is in quadrant III ?

   E. heart
   F. square
   G. circle
   H. star

Difficulty: Moderate

4. What shape is in quadrant II ?

   A. square
   B. star
   C. heart
   D. circle

Difficulty: Moderate

5. On a coordinate plane, You start at (1, 9). You move up 1 unit. Where do you end?

   E. (10, 1)   **G.** (-1, 10)
   F. (1, 10)   **H.** (0, 10)

Difficulty: Hard

6. On a coordinate plane, You start at (2, 3). You move to the right 2 units. Where do you end?

   A. (2, 5)   **C.** (2, 3)
   B. (0, 5)   **D.** (4, 3)

Difficulty: Hard

7. On a coordinate plane, you start at (7, 5). You move up 5 units. Where do you end?

   E. (7, 10) **G.** (7, 0)

   F. (12, 5) **H.** (2, 5)

   Difficulty: Hard

8. On a coordinate plane, you start at (1, 8). You move to the left 4 units. Where do you end?

   A. (1, 5) **C.** (-4, 8)

   B. (-3, 8) **D.** (1, -4)

   Difficulty: Hard

9. The coordinate plane is formed by a horizontal number line called the _____.

   E. y-axis
   F. x-axis
   G. coordinate plane
   H. ordered pair

   Difficulty: Moderate

10. The coordinate plane is formed by a vertical number line called the _____.

    A. y-axis
    B. x-axis
    C. coordinate plane
    D. ordered pair

    Difficulty: Moderate

11. A(n) _____ (x,y) describes the location of a point on the coordinate plane.

    E. y-coordinate
    F. x-coordinate
    G. coordinate plane
    H. ordered pair

    Difficulty: Moderate

12. The first number in an ordered pair is called the _____.

    A. x-coordinate
    B. x-axis
    C. coordinate plane
    D. ordered pair

    Difficulty: Moderate

13. The point where the axes meet is called the _____.

    E. axis **G.** origin

    F. coordinate **H.** endpoint

    Difficulty: Moderate

1. What name best describes this shape?

A. square
B. kite
C. quadrilateral
D. rectangle

Difficulty: Moderate

2. How many right angles does this quadrilateral have?

E. 2   G. 6
F. 4   H. 0

Difficulty: Moderate

3. What name best describes this shape?

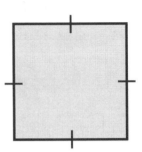

A. square   C. kite
B. trapezoid   D. triangle

Difficulty: Hard

4. What name best describes this shape?

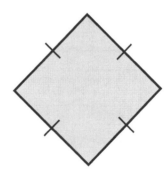

E. rectangle
F. square
G. trapezoid
H. pentagon

Difficulty: Hard

5. What name best describes this shape?

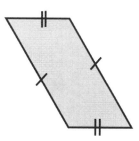

A. square
B. parallelogram
C. rectangle
D. triangle

Difficulty: Hard

6. What name best describes this shape?

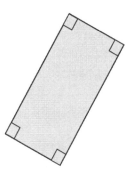

E. square
F. trapezoid
G. rectangle
H. triangle

Difficulty: Hard

7. What name best describes this shape?

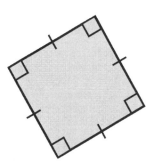

A. square
B. trapezoid
C. rectangle
D. triangle

Difficulty: Moderate

8. What name best describes this shape?

E. rhombus
F. trapezoid
G. quadrilateral
H. square

Difficulty: Hard

1. What name best describes this shape?

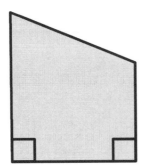

A. rhombus
B. trapezoid
C. rectangle
D. square

Difficulty: Hard

2. The name best that describes this shape is a _____.

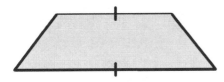

E. rectangle
F. square
G. rhombus
H. trapezoid

Difficulty: Hard

3. The name that best describes this shape is a _____ .

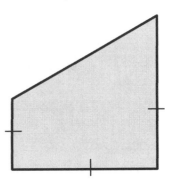

A. quadrilateral
B. square
C. rectangle
D. rhombus

Difficulty: Hard

4. The name that best describes the shape of this flag is the _____.

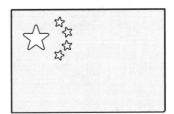

E. rectangle
F. rhombus
G. square
H. trapezoid

Difficulty: Hard

BRAIN HUNTER

5. The name that best describes this shape is _____ .

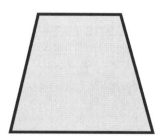

A. trapezoid
B. rhombus
C. square
D. kite

Difficulty: **Moderate**

6. What name best describes this shape?

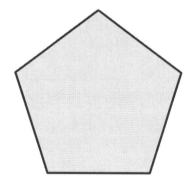

E. Parallelogram
F. Quadrilateral
G. Pentagon
H. Heptagon

Difficulty: **Moderate**

7. What name best describes this shape?

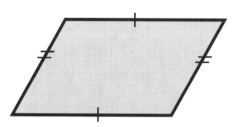

A. Heptagon
B. Pentagon
C. Square
D. Parallelogram

Difficulty: **Moderate**

8. What name best describes this shape?

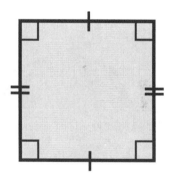

E. square
F. rectangle
G. rhombus
H. trapezoid

Difficulty: **Moderate**

9. What name best describes this shape?

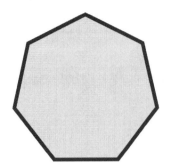

A. octagon
B. hexagon
C. pentagon
D. heptagon

Difficulty: Moderate

10. What name best describes this shape?

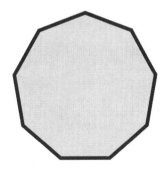

E. hexagon
F. nonagon
G. heptagon
H. pentagon

Difficulty: Moderate

11. Which choice(s) best apply to the statement: is a quadrilateral; does not have 4 right angles but does have two sets of opposite angles the same degree?

A. Rhombus
B. Rectangle
C. Trapezoid
D. Kite

Difficulty: Hard

12. Which choice(s) best applies to the statement: Is a quadrilateral. Has no parallel lines.

E. Square
F. Kite
G. Rectangle
H. Parallelogram

Difficulty: Hard

13. Which choice(s) best apply to the statement: Is a quadrilateral. Does not have 4 right angles but two sets of opposite angles the same degree. Also has 4 sides of equal length.

A. Kite
B. Square
C. Rhombus
D. Parallelogram

Difficulty: Hard

1. Which choice(s) best apply to the statement: Is a quadrilateral. Has only one pair of parallel sides.

   E. Parallelogram
   F. Rhombus
   G. Rectangle
   H. Trapezoid

   Difficulty: Hard

2. Which choice(s) best apply to the statement: Is a quadrilateral. Has 4 angles that are 90°.

   A. Kite
   B. Rectangle
   C. Trapezoid
   D. Square

   Difficulty: Hard

3. Which choice(s) best apply to the statement: Is a quadrilateral. Has 4 angles that are 90° and has 4 sides of equal length.

   E. Trapezoid
   F. Kite
   G. Square
   H. Rhombus

   Difficulty: Hard

4. Which choice(s) best apply to the statement: Is a quadrilateral.

   A. Rhombus
   B. Kite
   C. Parallelogram
   D. Rectangle

   Difficulty: Hard

5. Which choice(s) best apply to the statement: Is a quadrilateral. Does not have 4 right angles, but two sets of opposite angles the same degree.

   E. Trapezoid
   F. Rectangle
   G. Rhombus
   H. Parallelogram

   Difficulty: Hard

6. How many sides does a nonagon have?

   A. 9   **C.** 0
   B. 10   **D.** 7

   Difficulty: Easy

7. How many sides does a heptagon have?

E. 6   G. 3

F. 7   H. 11

Difficulty: Easy

8. What type of a polygon is this?

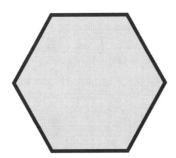

A. hexagon   C. octagon

B. heptagon   D. nonagon

Difficulty: Moderate

9. How many sides does an octagon have?

E. 7   G. 8

F. 6   H. 10

Difficulty: Easy

10. How many sides does a quadrilateral have?

A. 6   C. 4

B. 7   D. 3

Difficulty: Easy

11. Sandra was doing a craft project where she cut a piece of paper into a shape with 7 sides. What is the name of this shape?

E. triangle   G. octagon

F. heptagon   H. hexagon

Difficulty: Moderate

12. Petru's family is building a pool in the shape of a nonagon. How many sides will the pool have?

A. 6   C. 8

B. 7   D. 9

Difficulty: Moderate

13. Isaac's family is building a pool in the shape of a decagon. How many sides will the pool have?

E. 6   G. 10

F. 8   H. 12

Difficulty: Moderate

1. Gretchen sketched a logo into the shape of a pentagon. How many sides would the logo have?

   E. 5   G. 6
   F. 10   H. 3

   Difficulty: Moderate

2. A stained glass window is made of hundreds of tiny heptagons. How many sides would each heptagon have?

   A. 5   C. 7
   B. 6   D. 8

   Difficulty: Moderate

3. The patterns on a soccer ball are hexagons and pentagons. How many sides does the hexagon portion have?

   E. 4   G. 8
   F. 6   H. 10

   Difficulty: Moderate

4. Felix heard that a shape with 3 sides has angles that will always equal 180°. What shape did he learn about?

   A. hexagon   C. triangle
   B. pentagon   D. rectangle

   Difficulty: Moderate

5. For an art project Elliot cut a sheet of paper into a shape with 4 sides, but none of them were the same length. What type of shape was the paper?

   E. trapezoid
   F. heptagon
   G. octagon
   H. quadrilateral

   Difficulty: Moderate

6. While reading a book about buildings, Anna saw a building with 6 sides. This building is an example of what shape?

   A. octagon   C. hexagon
   B. pentagon   D. heptagon

   Difficulty: Moderate

7. Billy was looking at coin shapes from other countries and found one with 10 sides. This coin is what shape?

   E. pentagon   G. decagon
   F. octagon   H. nonagon

   Difficulty: Moderate

8. The patterns on a soccer ball are pentagons and hexagons. How many sides does the pentagon portion have?

A. 3   **C.** 7

B. 5   **D.** 9

Difficulty: **Moderate**

9. Annalise noticed that a table top had **5** sides. Because it has **5** sides, the top of the table would be what shape?

E. hexagon   **G.** octagon

F. pentagon   **H.** nonagon

Difficulty: **Moderate**

10. Teagen bought a poster with 4 equal length sides. What shape was the poster she bought?

A. square   **C.** trapezoid

B. rectangle   **D.** rhombus

Difficulty: **Moderate**

11. While drawing on some scrap paper, Xavier drew a shape with **9** sides. What is the name of this shape he drew?

E. hexagon   **G.** octagon

F. pentagon   **H.** nonagon

Difficulty: **Moderate**

12. Identify the type of quadrilateral shown below:

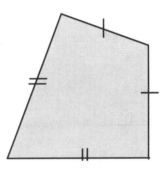

A. kite   **C.** rectangle

B. trapezoid   **D.** rhombus

Difficulty: **Moderate**

1. Identify the type of quadrilateral shown below:

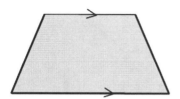

E. trapezoid   **G.** kite

F. rhombus   **H.** rectangle

Difficulty: Moderate

2. Identify the type of quadrilateral shown below:

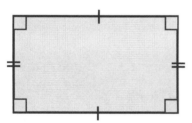

A. square   **C.** rectangle

B. rhombus   **D.** trapezoid

Difficulty: Moderate

3. Identify the type of quadrilateral shown below:

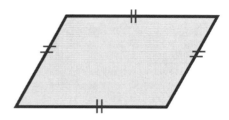

E. rectangle   **G.** rhombus

F. square   **H.** trapezoid

Difficulty: Moderate

4. Identify the type of quadrilateral shown below:

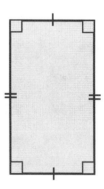

A. square   **C.** rhombus

B. kite   **D.** rectangle

Difficulty: Moderate

ANSWER SHEET

You can find detailed explanations
of each problem in the book by
visiting:
ArgoPrep.com/brain45

ARGOPREP

To see the answer explanations to the entire workbook, you can easily download the answer key from our website!

*Due to the high request from parents and teachers, we have removed the answer key from the workbook so you do not need to rip out the answer key while students work on the workbook.

All you need to do is:

Step 1 - Visit our website at: www.argoprep.com/brain45
Step 2 - You will see **DOWNLOAD ANSWER SHEETS** button.

⬇ **Download Answer Sheets**

Or scan the QR Code below:

Made in the USA
Middletown, DE
06 December 2023

44914795R00104